CW00540268

Shattering the (

SHATTERING THE GREAT DOUBT

The Chan Practice of Huatou

CHAN MASTER
Sheng Yen

SHAMBHALA
Boston & London
2009

SHAMBHALA PUBLICATIONS, INC.
HORTICULTURAL HALL
300 MASSACHUSETTS AVENUE
BOSTON, MASSACHUSETTS 02115
www.shambhala.com

9 8 7 6 5 4 3 2 1

First Edition

Printed in Canada
♾ This edition is printed on acid-free paper that meets
the American National Standards Institute z39.48 Standard.
♻ This book was printed on 100% postconsumer recycled
paper. For more information please visit
www.shambhala.com.
Distributed in the United States by Random House, Inc.,
and in Canada by Random House of Canada Ltd

LIBRARY OF CONGRESS CATALOGING-IN-PUBLICATION DATA
Shengyan, 1930–
Shattering the great doubt: the Chan practice of huatou /
Chan Master Sheng Yen.
p.   cm.
Includes index.
ISBN 978-1-59030-621-5
1. Spiritual life—Zen Buddhism.
2. Zen meditations. I. Title.
BQ9288.S518 2009
294.3'420427—dc22
2008044899

Contents

Contents

Editor's Preface

TWICE A YEAR between the fall of 1998 and the fall of 2006, Master Sheng Yen presented in the United States intensive retreats on the Chan practice of *huatou* (in Zen, *wato*). These retreats were held at the Dharma Drum Retreat Center in Pine Bush, New York. It was Master Sheng Yen's custom to give Dharma talks during the day on the practice of huatou, and in the evenings he commented on selected texts from ancient Chan masters on huatou practice. Given in Mandarin, these extemporaneous talks were concurrently translated into English and recorded. Thus, by the end of 2006, when Master Sheng Yen held what will most likely be his last huatou retreat in the West, the center had accumulated a considerable body of lectures on this one subject: how to practice this simple yet elusive meditative method of "seeing one's original face," that is to say, realizing one's innate wisdom.

When the decision was made to produce a book in English based on the master's teachings on huatou, it made sense to include both the first and the last of the series and to round them out with two more from in between. Therefore, we selected four retreats: the fall of 1998, the spring of 1999, the fall of 1999, and the fall of 2006. The first of these was a seven-day retreat, and the others, ten days long. It is our belief that these four retreats contain a full and definitive set of teachings by Master Sheng Yen on the method of huatou.

Since these four retreats represent some thirty-seven days of retreat lectures, with sometimes two or more per day, judicious selection from among the English transcripts was required to present the full depth and breadth of Master Sheng Yen's teaching on this method while keeping repetitions, albeit useful, to manageable limits. The result of this editorial process is a book in two parts: the first being selections from among the daytime lectures, and the second part, the evening commentaries in their entirety. (For historical accuracy, we provide sources that identify each chapter in the book by the retreat from which it came.)

We have not kept the chronological sequence of the daytime lectures in part 1, but instead have made an effort to present each lecture as a stand-alone teaching. At the same time the chapters follow a natural order from basics to matters of cultivation and attitude. In other words, there is no need or reason to read this book as if it were a manual on how to practice huatou, which in any case it is not. The selected lectures are presented here less as a journal and more as a tapestry of teachings woven from several strands of teachings on the same subject. Since they follow the text, the evening lectures in part 2 are in the original sequence.

Although this volume presents in detail both the reasons for and the methods by which one may practice huatou, to regard this book as a self-teaching manual would be a mistake. Rather, the intent is to present the method in all its simplicity and complexity as a resource for practitioners as well as teachers. For someone who has not practiced Chan or Zen in general or the huatou method in particular, a highly recommended starting point would be to find a Chan or Zen teacher who teaches the method.

In 2008, Master Sheng Yen announced his retirement from

traveling to the West and now lives and teaches at Dharma Drum Mountain, in Jinshan, Taiwan. We are indeed fortunate that while living in the United States, he gave us a legacy of precious teachings that includes, among many others, this book on huatou.

We are also deeply grateful to Shambhala Publications for bringing this volume to Western readers who are finding new horizons for spiritual growth in the ancient traditions that make up the Buddhist path.

Some Conventions Used in This Book

- The first occurrence of any term that is included in the glossary is preceded by an asterisk (*).
- The word *buddha* is capitalized when it refers to a specific buddha, such as Shakyamuni Buddha; otherwise it is lowercased. The same is true for the word *bodhisattva*. *Buddhadharma* is capitalized because it refers to the teachings of the historical Buddha, Shakyamuni.
- *Dharma* is capitalized when the context refers to the teachings of the Buddha. When lowercased, *dharmas* refer to phenomena, including objects of the mind.
- Diacritical marks are not used, as this volume is geared to a general audience. For example, *sūtra* is rendered as "sutra."
- Chinese terms are rendered using the Pinyin system of transliteration. Since pinyin does not separate conjoined characters with a hyphen, we have added an apostrophe when conjoining a word could cause confusion in its pronunciation: for example, *gong'an*. This is to avoid pronouncing the word wrongly as *gon gan*. To get a rough idea of the pronunciation of some of the common letters in Pinyin, please see the following simple guide:

c   pronounced like the English *ts*

q   pronounced like the English *ch*

x   pronounced like the English *hs*

zh pronounced like the English *j*

ERNEST HEAU
New York
2008

Acknowledgments

TEACHINGS: Chan Master Sheng Yen

ORAL TRANSLATION: Jimmy Yu (Guogu)

EDITING: Ernest Heau

EDITORIAL REVIEW: Jimmy Yu (Guogu)

TRANSCRIPTION: Bruce Rickenbacher, Stacey Polacco

PUBLICATION: Iris Wang

PART ONE

EXPOSITION
OF THE
HUATOU METHOD

THE HUATOU METHOD

Discovering Huatou

ALL THE TEACHINGS OF *CHAN have one purpose: liberation.
Yet, according to the styles of different Chan masters throughout
the ages, Chan was presented differently. Among all the Chan masters, it was the teachings of the sixth *patriarch Huineng (638–713)
that established the foundation of the tradition, even though his
teachings can be traced back to India through the Indian monk
*Bodhidharma (d. 536?), who was later named the first patriarch
of Chan. After Huineng, five historically significant Chan lineages
arose but only two survive: the *Caodong and the *Linji. In Japan,
Chan became Zen, the Caodong lineage became the Soto, and the
Linji lineage became the Rinzai. A popular conception of the *huatou method is that it is a distinct attribute of the Linji line and that
other Chan lines did not teach this method. This is a mistaken view,
at least for China. All lines used this method. However, it is safe to
say that it was Chan Master Dahui Zonggao (1089–1163) who gave it
its special place in the Chan tradition. At about the same time, Chan
Master Hongzhi Zhengjue (1091–1157) of the Caodong sect was
advocating Silent Illumination, although in his discourse records he

also seems to have used the huatou method. Through the transmissions of the lineage masters, both methods survive till today.

The huatou method is closely connected to the *gong'an*. The Japanese pronunciation of this term is *koan*, which means "public case," as in a legal case or events in the judicial system in premodern China. In Chan, a gong'an is an episode or case in the life of a Chan master, an episode that often bears directly upon the enlightenment of that master. Later, many gong'ans became subjects for practice, or investigation, by Chan practitioners. In actual practice, the entire gong'an is not always used because it can be complex and lengthy. Therefore, the early Chan masters would extract the essential point or the critical phrase or word from a gong'an and use it as a tool for practice. A huatou may consist of a fragment—a question or a word—derived from a gong'an. However, not all huatous are necessarily derived from gong'ans. Some are obscure in origin while others can simply be given by a master to a disciple as a method of practice.

Literally, *huatou* means "head, or crux, of a saying." A great modern Chinese master, Xuyun (1840–1959), explains a huatou as that which occurs just before a thought arises in your mind. To practice huatou the practitioner recites the sentence or fragment in a questioning manner but without theorizing or analyzing in order to find an answer. If you tried to reason out the meaning of a huatou, this would be looking at the tail end of the thought, not the head. In theory, to investigate the huatou means to examine that which occurs before thoughts arise. But what is that which lies before thoughts arise? What does the huatou point to? Our original, liberated mind. This is also called the "buddha-mind." To conceptually understand this is not enough; certainly it has no bearing on our vexations and life problems. You have to personally experience this. In practice, you must abandon concepts, knowledge, and previous experience until the huatou becomes the only thing in your mind, and you must eventually smash through the huatou itself.

Meditating on the Breath

When you first sit in meditation, your mind may be unsettled and you may have wandering thoughts. To calm your mind before taking up the huatou, you may practice breath meditation. You can do this by counting the breath or by following the breath. To count the breath, begin by relaxing and breathing naturally. Then starting with one, mentally count each exhalation until you reach ten, and then start all over with one. Repeat this cycle while experiencing the breath going in and out of your nose. If you lose the count, just go back to one and start all over again.

At some point you may become clearly aware of the breath going in and out without giving any numbers to it. If you can continue to do this, place your awareness at the tip of your nose, experiencing very clearly your breath going in and out. Or, you may also place your attention on the abdomen as it rises and falls with your breathing. At this point, you will be practicing following the breath. Of course, if you prefer, you can immediately practice following the breath without first practicing breath counting. However, for some people, beginning with breath counting is easier for calming the mind.

As you practice breath meditation, you may continue to have wandering thoughts. As soon as you become aware of this, just let go of the wandering thoughts and return to your breathing method. If this happens while counting the breath, just start counting again beginning with one. Eventually your wandering thoughts will taper off, your mind will be more settled, and you may begin practicing your huatou.

Reciting a Buddha's Name

Another simple method for settling the mind is to mentally recite the name of a buddha, such as *Amitabha, the Buddha of the Western Paradise. You could recite, "Homage to Amitabha Buddha," or in Chinese, "*Namo Amituofo.*" Recite at a moderate pace—too quickly may cause nervousness; too slowly may increase wandering thoughts or make you drowsy. You may also add a number after each recitation, for example, "*Namo Amituofo,* one; *Namo Amituofo,* two," and so on, to ten, and then repeat the cycle. However, focus on the words, not on the breath. Like working with the breath, the purpose of reciting a buddha's name is to reduce wandering thoughts and stabilize your mind.

To Know Yourself

To practice Chan is to know oneself, and knowing oneself, one will be able to ultimately liberate oneself. But knowing the self is difficult, having control of the self is more difficult, and liberating the self even more difficult. Yet, it must be done because all ignorance and afflictions arise from not knowing who we are. Lacking control of ourselves, we have vexations, we have self-grasping, and we are thus in bondage to the self. The purpose of practice is to liberate ourselves from this bondage. To do this, we need concepts as our guide and we need a method of practice.

The basic understanding of Chan is that our sense of self arises from the interactions of the body, mind, and external environment. In terms of methods, the first principle is to detach from the sense of self that arises from the external environment, then to detach from the sense of self that arises from our body, and lastly, to detach from the sense of self that arises from the activities of our mind. The latter includes sensations, feelings, ideas, and thoughts, which are essentially all attachments. So, step-by-step, you separate, isolate, and narrow down the sense of self. Until you do this, you will not be able to truly use the huatou method to ultimately shatter the sense of self and reach enlightenment.

Beginners often find it easy to gain an entry into the huatou method by identifying the sense of self that arises from our bodily sensations. For example, be aware of the weight of your body sitting in meditation; be aware of the breath passing through your nostrils, and so on. These sensations are all feelings of pleasure or discomfort that you can recognize. Your awareness of these sensations is an aspect of the sense of self. Who is experiencing these things? That is what I mean by a "sense of self"—identifying the "who" that is aware, the "who" that is experiencing. So once this sense of self is identified, stay with it; do not allow the mind to wander. Stay with sensing and being aware; let your body be the anchor to keep the mind from floating away. For today, use this method to become clear about the self. However, if your mind is already concentrated and calm and you have no strong sense of self, then you can right away begin using huatou. Otherwise, if your body is still prominent in your mind, then practice watching your sensations for today.

There is no need to use a full-lotus or a half-lotus posture; just choose a posture that is comfortable for sitting so long as your body is upright. Relax the body and be aware of your breath going in and out. Through awareness of your breath, you will know and experience your own existence. You exist because of your breath, and you will have that so long as you are alive. So stay with the awareness of your breath. Doing this, you gain a sense of your own being. As you continue, your breath will slow down, become deeper, and sink lower. At that time, you may become aware of the rise and fall of your abdomen. Let that process happen naturally. Be aware of it, but do not think about it. Practicing like this, you will gain in concentration and steadiness and you may feel comfortable. Stay close to the awareness of your sense of self. If you do that, after some time you will be able to use the huatou method.

To relax your body, first, relax your eyes, your facial muscles, and your head. Then, make sure your shoulders and arms are relaxed, then your chest, back, and lower back. While maintaining an erect posture, be sure your lower abdomen is also relaxed. If you can maintain these basic points of a relaxed body, your breath will be smooth and unhindered. However, if any part of your body is tense, your breath will be short and constricted. If you relax your body in the manner I just said, your breath will naturally be smooth and unhindered; you will experience the rise and fall of your abdomen, and the breath will naturally sink down.

So, relax the body and be aware of your sense of self from one moment to the next. You do this by paying attention to the breath. If you catch your mind wandering, come back to your breath. Detach from the environment; pay no attention to it. If you get involved in things heard and seen, you will be overwhelmed by wandering thoughts. Just stay with your experience of this very moment, moment to moment, one instant to the next. And what is this present experience? It is your sense of self grounded in awareness of the body or the mind.

Like the Two Wings of a Bird

All meditation practices aim to first stabilize and harmonize the mind. This is not easy to do. When we meditate, to outward appearances we may be sitting still but inwardly our mind may be quite busy. The outward physical calm may conceal a scattered mind. Correct Chan practice can be likened to the wings of a bird: the first wing would be the guiding concepts; the second wing would be the methods of practice. Just as a bird needs both wings to fly, only when we have both the correct concepts as well as suitable methods can we really practice Chan. Therefore our aim is to gain a correct understanding of Chan concepts and also to practice the huatou method. When the mind is supremely calm and no vexations are present, it becomes open and spacious; it can then manifest its natural state, which is that of wisdom. When the mind is replete with wisdom, this can be called "enlightenment."

To practice huatou, you repeatedly ask in your mind a single question with an urgent desire for an answer but without relying on thinking. What kind of question? Questions such as "What is *wu*?"

"Who is dragging this corpse around?" and "What was my *original face before I was born?" You can even have a huatou with just one word, for example, "*Wu?*"

Ask the huatou to the exclusion of all other thoughts until the question is resolved. The crucial point is that the question cannot be resolved by logical or conceptual thinking. After you have chosen or have been assigned a huatou, you should just stick with it. Constantly switching your huatou makes it difficult to generate consistent power. In fact, you can practice the same huatou all your life, even after you have experienced an initial enlightenment. You can use the huatou to experience enlightenment again and again until you are thoroughly enlightened. I highly recommend that you use the huatou "What is *wu?*" as this is a very powerful one that has been used since the early days of this practice.

When you start to sit in meditation, you can directly enter the practice by energetically asking your question over and over. For example, in your mind you would ask, "What is *wu?* What is *wu?* What is *wu?*" You must direct the asking to the huatou, not to yourself. Continue at a moderate pace, and always ask with a questioning mind; let your mind settle into the method; become friends with it. When there is nothing in your mind but finding the answer, this is called "investigating huatou." This is how huatou should be practiced.

When you engage the huatou, avoid analyzing it. The proper approach is to just ask the question and let the huatou itself give the answer. With this attitude, you just keep asking the huatou. Do not turn that around and start asking *yourself,* expecting the answer to come from you. That will start you thinking, and you may end up with a stuffy head. If you direct the question to yourself, you may get answers from your subconscious, but they will invariably be wrong because they will be conceptual. If this happens, just let these false answers go. Say to yourself, "This is not the answer I'm looking for," and continue to ask the huatou.

Neither is a huatou a mantra to be recited over and over without a questioning mind. As for the questioning, do not add second thoughts. Clever people may wonder how you can get a Chan experience from asking a question that has no meaning. "How can asking 'What is *wu*?' make me enlightened?" If you think like this, it is because you lack faith and confidence, and in that case, the huatou will not work for you. Rather, just look at the huatou as a tool for practicing Chan. Just directly go about it this way: keep asking the huatou and let it give you the answer. The point of this method is not only to allow your mind to focus on the huatou, but also to give rise to a sense of wanting to find an answer. These factors—focusing the mind and wanting an answer—force your self-centeredness into a corner, so to speak. By your persistent questioning, the self eventually has nowhere to go and vanishes. When the self vanishes, the answer you were looking for will manifest by itself and you will come to know personally the state of liberation.

While asking the huatou, you will have wandering thoughts. As soon as you become aware of this, just pick up your huatou and continue to ask. This way, you are using the huatou to dispel wandering thoughts. There is a Chan saying that we should use the diamond sword of wisdom to cut through delusions. In fact, anything that manifests in your mind naturally disappears when you have this sword in hand. So think of the huatou as your diamond sword. Again and again you must ask the huatou; you must generate the desire for the huatou to give you an answer. Just keep asking the huatou and pick it up when wandering thoughts arise. Eventually, you will truly be investigating the huatou. At that point what we call the doubt sensation will arise, and eventually, it will evolve into a great mass of doubt. When the great doubt is shattered, you will have answered your huatou.

You must bear in mind two principles: first, do not analyze your huatou, since you will not get a correct answer that way; second, do not try to control your breath in any way, such as to suppress wandering thoughts. If you have wandering thoughts, just pick up the huatou, but don't connect it in any way with your breath.

The function of both huatou and gong'an is to generate what we call the "great doubt." This doubt does not mean skepticism or suspicion, but an intense uneasiness and wonderment that we must know the meaning of the huatou. It is a state of all-consuming questioning that is relentless, not settling for any solution other than the complete resolution of the huatou. Such resolution means liberation from the great matter of birth and death. Naturally there are degrees of the doubt, from momentary feelings of a fleeting doubt sensation, to a persistent undercurrent of the doubt in all of your daily activities, to a great doubt sensation where you feel your whole world has collapsed into this sense of intense wonderment. When the doubt reaches a crescendo, it becomes vast and self-sustaining. Under certain circumstances this great doubt will explode; your sense of self will suddenly vanish and enlightenment will occur. The huatou is a great tool, and you must generate the doubt by investigating it.

In the Chan tradition there have been many commonly used huatous, but in my retreats I have found four to be useful, effective, and direct. The first of these is "What is *wu*?" This huatou is based on an encounter in which a disciple asked Master Zhaozhou (778–897), "Does a dog have buddha-nature?" The master answered, "*Wu*," which means "no," "nothing," or "without." This paradoxical exchange is perhaps the best-known gong'an in the history of Chan. There is more elaboration of this gong'an in the section on "*Wu* and Buddha-Nature" on page 143.

A second often-used huatou is "Who is dragging this corpse around?" The corpse here is our own physical body, but why a corpse? Without a "spirit" to give life to our body, it would just be a corpse. But if you use this huatou, do not speculate on what it means. Just ask, "Who is dragging this corpse around?"

A third common huatou derives from the teaching that *sentient beings transmigrate from one life to another in *samsara, the cycle of birth and death. Do you know what form you had before being born as a sentient being? So, you ask, "What was my original face before birth and death?" Like any other huatou, just keep asking the question and engage it again if you lose it.

The fourth huatou I am going to mention is popular among Chinese Buddhists who practice mindfulness by reciting the Buddha's name. Without turning up a second thought or straying off for some answer, directly ask, "Who is reciting the Buddha's name?" Another version of the same huatou is, "Who is mindful of the Buddha?"

Among the four huatous I have mentioned here, the one I have found most effective and direct for students is, "What is *wu*?" But if you have trouble using this one, you may use any of the others for your huatou practice. So I encourage most people to use "What is *wu*?" or just "*Wu*?" For those who cannot connect with the Chinese *wu*, you can simply use the English "What is nothingness?" Not only does this huatou not have any side effects, it is the most direct and simple huatou that you can use. So, if you can use "What is *wu*?" that is fine. If not, ask, "What is nothingness?"

In the West, "Who am I?" is another popular huatou that is not traditional in the Chan tradition. I do not encourage people to use this, because it puts an "I" at the center of this question and some may find it difficult to drop this "I."

"What Is Wu?"

"What is *wu*?" is the huatou I usually recommend. *Wu* is the state where the sense of self is totally absent; it is the state of no-self. "No-self" means there is no abiding, unchanging entity that you can identify as "I." This no-self is the natural state of enlightenment.

Now, understanding no-self in this way is insufficient because enlightenment must be personally experienced. To experience no-self personally, you ask, "What is *wu*?" putting your whole life behind the question. It does not mean becoming tense, anxious, or nervous. It just means asking the huatou with utmost sincerity and single-mindedness. So, with this attitude, you ask, "What is *wu*?" At the same time, don't fall into the trap of becoming tense. If you become physically tense, your whole body will stiffen, your breathing will be constricted, and you will feel pressure in your chest. If you become mentally tense, you will become exhausted, fall into drowsiness, or stir up wandering thoughts. So, without tension in body or mind, put your whole focus into asking the huatou. That is how to investigate your huatou.

Stages of Huatou Practice

Huatou can be practiced at three levels, or stages: reciting the huatou, asking the huatou, and investigating the huatou.

The first stage, reciting the huatou, is quite simple—you just mentally recite the words of the huatou, over and over. At this stage you may not feel the urgency of knowing the answer, of discovering the meaning of the huatou. You are simply reciting it somewhat like a mantra, over and over, or like reciting the name of a buddha. At this level it is common to still have a lot of wandering thoughts. Even so, if you persist, it will still be useful for calming and settling the mind.

The second stage, asking the huatou, is accompanied by a great desire to know the answer. You are no longer simply reciting the huatou, but you sincerely want to know the answer. At that time you also feel a great attraction or interest in the huatou. You are drawn to the huatou, and because of that, your wandering thoughts will diminish to a great extent. As wandering thoughts fade, even though you are not yet at one with the huatou, you will still be able to generate power in the practice. At this point, you are still in opposition to this huatou, meaning you are clearly separate from it; you are the one asking the huatou, and the huatou is being asked by you. What sustains this power is your strong urgency in wanting to know the answer.

At the third stage, investigating the huatou, you are no longer separate from the huatou but have become one with it. In fact, you are completely engulfed by the asking. Although "What is *wu*?" may still be there, eventually it will also disappear, leaving you with just a deep sense of wonderment that we call the "doubt sensation." Doubt here does not mean suspicion. It simply means a desire to know the answer; it is a mind of questioning and wonderment. In the midst of that, you are completely one with this doubt sensation. At a shallow level you are still asking "What is *wu*?" but when you become completely engulfed in the doubt, the asking itself disappears and there is just this state of wonderment. You can sit, stand, walk, and sleep. You may lose track of space and time, yet you can still function, but your whole being is permeated by this wanting to know, this doubt and great wonderment. You have generated what is called in Chan the "great doubt mass." Some practitioners are able to be in this state for a few hours, some for several days, and some for longer periods. Chan Master Laiguo (1881–1953) was in this state for three whole months.

The whole point of the huatou method is to generate the doubt sensation. There is the saying, "Great doubt, great enlightenment; small doubt, small enlightenment; no doubt, no enlightenment." This says that the depth of any realization will correspond to the power of one's doubt. If you nurture doubt into a great mass only to have it dissipate shortly after, then you may gain only a very shallow realization. However, if one generates a great doubt mass that lasts for days or longer, a subsequent breakthrough would be much greater. Indeed it could last a lifetime.

How does one go from merely reciting, to asking, and then to investigating their huatou? The keys to this are interest, urgency, and confidence. You must have great interest in working with your huatou. Why should you? Well, because you recognize that you bring afflictions upon yourself and others, all due to the lack of wisdom. With the desire to be free of afflictions, you will be able to generate interest in the huatou. With interest comes great urgency and sincere desire to resolve your existential conflicts. You must then also believe that giving rise to the doubt sensation will help you resolve your problems.

If you are unable to generate the doubt sensation, the practice is still useful for calming your mind. So, even without generating the doubt sensation, huatou is still useful. Just recite in your mind the huatou, steadily, without interruption, with a relaxed mind and body. Once your body and attitude are relaxed, your sole task is to stay with the huatou, not allowing yourself to stray away from it. "What is *wu*? What is *wu*? What is *wu*?" Just continue whether or not you have wandering thoughts. Just be clear that the huatou is on your mind as you repeat it. If you become aware of wandering thoughts, immediately return your attention to the huatou. If you are not having any wandering thoughts, then don't worry about anything else. Just stick to the huatou. So, continuously practicing like this, at the very least your mind will become settled and calm.

Why do I recommend that you use "What is *wu*?" or just "*Wu*?" when there are numerous huatous one can choose from? The answer is that among the huatous we have discussed, "*Wu*?" is the most clear-cut, the easiest to use, and the most effective; it is less likely to generate side effects or a whole host of thought-streams. Because "*Wu*?" is the most direct, the simplest, and also holds the most strength, Chan Master Dahui Zonggao advocated it, and I myself also encourage people to use it.

Just remember that any huatou is not a mantra; it a question that you ask instead of just reciting. If you do not feel intimate with the Chinese word *wu*, you can say it in English. So ask, "What is nothingness?" And since you are asking, "What is nothingness?" there is no further question that needs to be asked about what nothingness is. So whether you use *wu* or "nothingness," it is really just a symbol signifying an attitude of questioning deep down inside you.

Investigating Huatou

Practicing huatou is simple—all you do is ask the question that is your huatou. Do not involve yourself with anything else. This continual questioning is called "investigating the huatou." However, investigating the huatou does not mean trying to find the answer by thinking about it. In fact, any answer you come up with will be wrong. The answer must come from the huatou itself. For this reason, Chan Master Dahui Zonggao said that the proper way to practice huatou is to save your energy for when it will benefit the most. Just think! How simple it is to do nothing except ask, "What is *wu*?" And you don't even have to come up with the answer yourself—the huatou will do that. So, you just persist in this urgent asking as your single task: "What is *wu*?" Let yourself wake from drowsiness; let wandering thoughts stop; let your body relax. This is indeed a very easy, effortless method; but if you overexert, you will exhaust yourself, and if you try to think about an answer, it will be just delusion.

You may begin practicing huatou by being aware of your body and its sensations. Staying with your bodily awareness, do not allow your mind to wander off into the environment; you should experience your mind and body as one. If you are aware of your feelings and thoughts from moment to moment, you will become self-contained with a clear sense of self. Whether it is pain, drowsiness, wandering thoughts, or discomfort, tell yourself, "I am experiencing this." If you persist you will become more self-contained; your sense of self will stabilize and anchor your mind. Eventually you will realize that all your wandering thoughts and deluded thinking are contained in this single sense of self. At that point you are ready to use the huatou. However, if you still have problems settling into this clear sense of self, you may begin asking the huatou anyway. The main thing to remember is that it is an effortless approach; all you have to do is just stay with it from moment to moment.

Try to first settle into a clear sense of self before asking the huatou. If your mind is not settled, you can still ask the huatou but you will most likely be scattered and agitated. At such times patience is important. You are already disturbed by wandering thoughts, so you do not want to stir up more agitation. As soon as you are aware of wandering thoughts, just go back to the huatou. Use the same remedy for discomfort or restlessness—just return to the huatou. The thing to avoid is either seeking results or rejecting your situation, because either one will prevent your mind from settling. So, the first key is to be patient; the second key is to return to the method when you lose it. If you start by first settling into a clear sense of self, that is very good. If you can persist and abide in this sense of self, you will be able to practice huatou effectively. So, you can either let the mind settle first or go directly into asking the huatou. Either approach will take some practice.

Generating the Doubt Sensation

How do you generate the doubt sensation? You do it by continually asking the huatou with a sincere and urgent desire to know the answer. You can ask the huatou with intensity, or you can ask it in a more relaxed manner. People who are in good physical condition and have strong willpower can use the more intense approach; otherwise I recommend the more relaxed approach. In daily life the intense approach to huatou is difficult to do, so the relaxed approach is more suitable then. On the other hand, for a fixed period of time such as a retreat, it is more feasible to use a more intense approach. With either approach, one still should not use the mind to reason about the huatou.

The main difference between the intense and relaxed approaches is really one of attitude. The intense approach can be likened to the urgency of holding on to a log in the middle of the ocean; if you let go, you will drown. You should ask the huatou with that kind of urgency, knowing that only the huatou holds the answer. So, you must ask the huatou very intensely and very intently. Single-mindedly, you want to find out what *wu* is or whatever your huatou is. Continue to ask without giving up and with the utmost urgency. Imagine that if you give up for just one minute, you will die. With such intensity, wandering thoughts cannot arise because the practice is seamless, without gaps. With this intense approach you can benefit more and see results more quickly, but it can be dangerous.

The first danger with this intense approach is that you can start *thinking* about the huatou instead of simply *asking* the huatou; you will start using your mind on the huatou, and as this gets intense, you may get a headache or a stuffy head, dizziness, and so on. The second danger is that with such intensity, you may have strong expectations, and that mind-set will induce obstructions. We call these obstructions demonic because they arise from your own mind; they are really illusions or hallucinations that may arise in practice. The third danger of the intense approach is that you may try to synchronize your breath with the asking, or the asking may influence your pattern of breathing. This can lead to chills, tension, and other discomforts, thus hindering practice. These are the three general dangers that may arise when you use huatou intensely. However, those who are emotionally stable and confident are very welcome to use the intense approach.

In the relaxed approach, you also want to know the answer to the huatou, but you are not pushing too hard, looking for extraordinary experiences, or trying to get rid of anything. Single-mindedly, you just maintain the desire to find the answer. While this approach is more relaxed, it still needs to be seamless. By "seamless" we mean being mindful that with each asking of the huatou, wandering thoughts do not seep in. Relaxed yet mindful, you ask the huatou, develop interest in it, and you appreciate the asking of the huatou. This is like a puppy playing with a ball for a long time. Similarly, with this relaxed approach, you have to nourish the interest and appreciate the questioning, even play with the huatou. All this is done as if you were walking down a road holding a bowl filled to the brim with precious oil. Your job is not to spill a single drop of oil, so you must walk with utmost mindfulness. This mindfulness is being careful, not tense.

If you become fatigued using this relaxed approach, that is because your mind is hazy. As long as you can clearly hold the huatou, you can temporarily put the method aside and take a rest. After recovering your energy, pick up the huatou again. In daily life you can use a similar approach: in general, just be mindful and focused, and once in a while, pick up the huatou. And if you have some task at hand, you can put the huatou aside, finish the task single-mindedly and maintain concentration. When talking to people, you can do the same. After you've finished the task or conversation, you can pick up the huatou again and continue mindfully.

Although this kind of practice is relaxed, it is like dripping water that will eventually wear a hole in a rock. Similarly, when you practice this approach, after a long time you will find that your character has been refined and your mind has become very clear and spacious and is endlessly useful. Eventually and gradually your character becomes more refined and more stable, and your mind becomes clearer and more spacious. After some time your teacher may recognize that you have become enlightened without your being aware of it. In this case, the event occurred naturally and gradually, while your vexations diminished and your personality became more stable. Although enlightenment in this approach may not happen as abruptly and quickly as in the intense approach, it is possible. By contrast, in the intense approach, enlightenment can be reached more quickly but it comes with dangers, as we have discussed.

Even though the relaxed approach can lead to enlightenment, there is never a guarantee, and there are reasons for this. Some people practice very lazily, thinking they are seriously practicing. I return to the analogy of the bowl filled to the brim with oil. It is of no use if you are not walking because you are not making progress. The point is to continue to walk without spilling. Regardless of how slow you are walking, you still walk with full mindfulness, giving yourself enough time to reach the goal without hurrying. If you have to put down the bowl every time you get a little tired or bored, that is being lazy and you will have difficulty making progress. Therefore, the point of this relaxed approach is to practice continually but with an attitude of nonseeking.

Whether you take an intense or relaxed approach, please practice with diligence. Those of you who are not using the huatou can still use the analogy of walking with a full bowl. With very careful mindfulness, use whatever method you are using. No matter which approach you take, practice very carefully and attentively, making sure no wandering thought seeps in. When there is only the huatou in your mind, you can give rise to a questioning attitude. Then, naturally, the doubt sensation will arise and you will be able to generate a great mass of doubt. If there are wandering thoughts, it will be difficult for the doubt sensation to arise.

Body and Mind Phenomena

Most practitioners at one time or another will experience physical or psychological reactions during meditation. The reactions can be pain, soreness, numbness, itchiness, as well as involuntary movements, such as shaking or rocking. Your body may experience warmth or coolness, extreme heat or cold. Psychological reactions from intense practice consist mostly of illusions and vexations.

Auditory illusions are sounds heard only by the person experiencing them. They could even be based on real events that happened before but are being replayed in one's mind, like the meditation bells or the chanting service. Visual illusions can come when gazing steadily at something and patterns start to appear. Or they can be scenes and images seen when your eyes are closed, which you take for real. When these visual illusions occur, open your eyes wide and try not to focus too hard on objects. It is also possible to experience scents and aromas, often triggered by memory. Tactile sensations can lead to a whole variety of illusions, but they are not necessarily based on physical contact. They can be very general sensations, such as a dry feeling on the skin, or the body may feel very supple or very tense. Other types of bodily illusion are feeling like the body is expanding or shrinking, floating or sinking. All of these are illusions and should be ignored. Open your eyes wide and continue with the method you are practicing.

Illusions can also arise from a mind of greed and aversion, of liking and disliking; in other words, from a mind that seeks special experiences. Aversion is the mind of trying to avoid or suppress certain kinds of experiences. When you have a mind of seeking or avoiding things, psychological reactions will occur and illusions will manifest.

These are common physical and psychological reactions from intense practice. If you experience them, fine; if not, it's also fine. Continue to practice; and if you experience them, since you have paid attention to what I have said, naturally you'll know what to do.

The Meaning of Huatou Practice

When Master Xuyun gave *Dharma talks he sometimes apologized to his disciples. He was contrite about interrupting their practice, but as retreat master, he felt obliged to speak the Dharma. Since I am ill, I too feel that perhaps this retreat master should not talk.

But like Xuyun, if I did not teach Dharma, I would not live up to your expectations. Actually whether I talk or not, either would be appropriate.

In fact, when I speak the Dharma all you have to do is listen with your ears, while in your heart you should continue to practice. Are you able to do this? Isn't it better to single-mindedly work on your huatou instead of listening to my ramblings? Or perhaps while practicing you can allow some of this stuff to mingle with the huatou. If this Dharma talk is just rambling, wouldn't it be wonderful to ignore it and just work on the huatou? Or perhaps precisely because your mind is full of wandering thoughts, you need more wandering thoughts to help you practice. And finally, since all thoughts are just discursive thinking, why do we need more discursive thinking?

Chan Master Zhaozhou once said that during the twenty-four hours in a day his mind was not complicated by extraneous thoughts. This is indeed impressive, because not only did he practice while sitting but also while interacting with people. He was not just walking around like a zombie but dealing with complex affairs. Ordinary people can practice single-mindedly while awake, but it is highly unlikely that they can practice while asleep.

Another Chan master, Gaofeng Yuanmiao (1238–95), once told his disciples, "If you can practice continuously for seven days straight, I guarantee that you will be enlightened; if not, you can chop off my head." This story became a gong'an that Master Xuyun used because no one has been able to disprove Master Gaofeng's assertion. Indeed, if you can practice huatou for seven days continuously, seamlessly, without any gaps, and with utter clarity, after seven days and seven nights, you *should* be enlightened.

If you were to ask yourself why you cannot practice without a gap for seven straight days, the answer will be that you lack determination. In Buddhist terms this is "lacking the great vow." Lacking determination, it is so easy for you to be interrupted by wandering thoughts, sounds in the environment, bodily discomfort, this or that. But if you can will yourself to stick to the method from moment to moment, no matter what, the more confident you will grow. Conversely, the more confident you are, the stronger your determination will grow. Lacking determination to begin with, what should you do? You should vow again and again to not stray from the method. And if you discover you have strayed off, pull yourself back to the method. If you make this vow at each sitting, in time your mind will become accustomed to sticking to the method. You will be able to restfully use your huatou without interruption, seamlessly, without gaps.

However, if you just bring forth the huatou without generating doubt, that is no different from just repeating a mantra. At most it will pacify the mind. So doubt is essential. When you bring forth the huatou, you must at the same time arouse doubt. If you persist, you will eventually generate what is called a "great doubt mass." But I remind you that great doubt does not guarantee enlightenment, let alone no doubt whatsoever. The idea is to continuously pick up *wu,* arouse the doubt that can eventually grow into the great ball of doubt, and then shatter that great doubt. But if you sit there with your mind at ease—sometimes *wu* is there, sometimes not—you are not investigating huatou. The skill lies in being taut, that is to say, without gaps, while being relaxed in body and mind. So train yourself to practice huatou continuously and without effort. This is the course of practice with huatou.

Although huatou has been practiced for centuries, it was not until the modern age that Master Xuyun explained the term "huatou." Xuyun said that the purpose of practicing huatou is to illuminate our mind so that we can see our true self-nature. But what is true self-nature? It is none other than buddha-nature. What is buddha-nature? Buddha-nature is emptiness. What is emptiness? Surely, emptiness is not a void where there are no objects, nor is it a kind of lack. This emptiness is what underlies the reality of what it is to be a sentient being, what it is to be a buddha. Emptiness is the buddha-nature that lies within each of us as our intrinsic nature. Therefore to investigate Chan is to investigate the minds of sentient beings, to investigate buddha-nature. To know the mind of sentient beings is precisely to know the mind of a buddha. So, minds, sentient beings, and Buddha are one.

How does this relate to the huatou? The Chinese word *hua* means "words," sometimes translated as "spoken words," expressed either mentally or externally. The word *tou* can mean "head," "bud," "wellspring," or "source." What is the wellspring of spoken words? Or simply put, what are spoken words? Spoken words are symbols we use to communicate, to think. What lies behind these symbols? What lies behind is the source or wellspring. This wellspring is not some object or some original place from which these symbols come; rather it is precisely emptiness. This emptiness is not something lacking or vacant as in a void. It is actually quite full in that it embodies both sentient beings and buddhas.

So, the relationship between huatou, Chan, and buddha-nature is that we investigate the source of the spoken words, which is none other than our own buddha-mind. This mind is the mind of emptiness, our true buddha-nature. We cannot investigate this directly because it is not a knowable object external to us. If that were the case, it would be in opposition to us. Therefore, the method of huatou is to use symbols to investigate the source of symbols. But Master Xuyun said that when we utter the huatou, it is no longer in the wellspring. Once we utter *wu*, it is already the "tail" of that thought. But since the "head" or source of the thought cannot be known objectively, we use the tail to know it. So asking *wu* is like chasing the tail; we use it to investigate the mind, which is to say, our true buddha-nature.

You don't need an explanation of the huatou method to use it. I am giving it so that you may know that there is a reason behind the method and how it relates to investigating Chan. Now we have time for a couple of questions.

Student: At one time during the day I felt as if a door had suddenly been opened and I was able to plunge myself into the huatou, which was clearly present. I was able to perceive the external environment, but it was no longer a burden, just a kind of distant light. There were thoughts coming and going, but they lacked power. As soon as they arose, I felt a force sweeping them away and I was able to continue with the huatou.

Sheng Yen: This is a good experience, but it lacks the doubt. You may have had doubt, but it was not strong enough to persist. Tell yourself, "It's no big deal." Say, "That's not what I want, but what *do* I want? I don't know." Just work on the huatou, arouse this "not knowing." "What is *wu*? I don't know but I *want* to know." Do not have any fixed idea about what it is you want to know, but whatever comes up tell yourself, "That's not it." Persisting in *wu* while not knowing is how to generate the doubt. Experiences like yours will arise, but it is not deep enough. Just continue with the method.

Student: I am having trouble with the huatou because my past experiences with the breath-following method keep coming back. What should I do?

Sheng Yen: Right now you are using the huatou method, so if anything comes back from your past experience, just let it go and continue with the huatou. Of course, out of habit, you will come back to the breath method again and again. So the only way is to retrain yourself. When the older habit returns, just drop it and continue with the huatou, again and again. In time you will be able to stay with the huatou. Otherwise for the rest of your life you will not be able to use another method.

Direct Contemplation

In an intense Chan retreat context, you must use the huatou method all the time, even during walking meditation. Walking meditation is actually a chance to practice huatou in daily life. However, you may notice the sounds and forms in your environment when walking. If you have already generated the doubt sensation, these perceptions will not disturb you and you should just persist in the huatou. However, if you're disturbed by them, you can use a method called "direct contemplation" to help you settle the mind. In this method you train your mind to directly perceive what is in front of you, using just your eyes or ears. The main point is to not engage in discriminatory thought. So, there are three principles: do not label, do not describe, do not compare. Just allow whatever is in front of you to be perceived as it is. That is direct contemplation.

When you do this well, you can then progress to contemplating emptiness. Contemplation in popular usage means "thinking," "reflecting," or "analyzing." However, in Buddhism, contemplating emptiness, for example, does not mean thinking about emptiness. Contemplation is just a nonconceptual way of perception, allowing the mind to abide in a certain state. How does one go from direct contemplation to contemplating emptiness? In direct contemplation there should be nothing on your mind besides the objects you perceive. With no concepts, labels, or comparisons attached, the mind can perceive the object as it is. Though you might persist in this state for a long time, it is still not enlightenment because there is an "I" perceiving and an object being perceived.

After becoming adept at this practice, your mind learns how to maintain its clarity without fixing on the object of meditation. At this point you are beginning to contemplate emptiness. To contemplate emptiness, do not let the mind fix on the form or sound of objects; do not fix on external events or situations, and do not fix on internal thoughts or ideas. So, internally as well as externally, do not allow the mind to rest anywhere. Many thoughts will arise within you, and you will perceive many things outside, but let the mind detach from all that. Unlike direct contemplation where you let your mind rest on, say, a sound, now you just let it go. Do not allow the free flow of the mind to be caught up with your perceptions. If you see forms, do not allow them to become the contents of your mind; just let them go. Similarly with internal thought and concepts—let them go. Though many things can come up, you are simply in a state of nonabiding, of letting go. So, stay with that process of experiencing, then letting go. It is a continual process of merely noticing, in which things present themselves to your field of awareness and then vanish of their own accord. If you do this very well, it is possible to bypass shattering of the great mass of doubt and still experience enlightenment. This method is not easy, but it is also not hard.

So, you have three methods: huatou, direct contemplation, and contemplating emptiness. All of you are familiar with at least huatou. Second, you have direct contemplation—no labeling, no describing, no comparing. And third is contemplation of emptiness, letting go of whatever you experience. This last is just a side dish to entice you to try it! Do not entertain self-disparaging thoughts. Sometimes people have a lot of vexations, and, all of a sudden, these vexations can clear up and suddenly the mind is at peace. So, have confidence in yourself and do this practice.

CULTIVATION

The Meaning of Cultivation

IN CHAN, we speak of "cultivation." The Chinese term *xiuxing*, sometimes translated as "practice," connotes rectifying, correcting, or amending. In cultivating Chan, we are trying to rectify our erroneous ways. We begin by recognizing errors in our way of acting, thinking, or speaking; we become aware of aspects in our behavior that are troubling to ourselves as well as to others. This is the real meaning of cultivation. But recognizing our shortcomings is not easy, much less correcting them. Cultivating harmlessness is more than just recognizing our mistakes. Each stage of cultivation is harder than the previous: first, we must recognize our mistakes; second, we must rectify them; and third, we must become free of negativities that cause harm.

To begin self-discovery we can use the methods of Chan, but we first need to recognize the negativities of body, speech, and mind. With regard to speech, we should be aware when our words are unkind and hurtful; with regard to the body, we must admit that we do things that cause harm; and with regard to the mind, we must recognize attitudes, habits, and vexations that are unwholesome. Therefore, practice should be a holistic approach to rectifying our whole being. Sitting still in meditation, we may at best recognize certain unwholesome mental habits; we may also become aware of discomfort and other physical vexations. However, real cultivation goes beyond sitting in meditation, so we need to extend it to our interactions with others, which is harder.

In the midst of practice, you may experience negative mental states. The most common of these arise from the three poisons—the *kleshas,* or afflictions of desire, aversion, and ignorance. When your practice is not going well, you will often recognize resentment, anger, dislike, and so on. When meditation is going smoothly, it is harder to recognize subtler vexations, since your mind will tend to smooth over them. On the other hand, when meditation is going very well and you experience bliss, you may succumb to the poison of desire and attach to the bliss. Any of these states, pleasant or unpleasant, are vexations of the mind.

When we reflect on it, we realize that sometimes we speak when the situation does not call for it, but when the situation does call for speech, we say the wrong things. We may even realize that we have always been doing this. As for acting, sometimes a response from us is not needed and yet we act, causing problems. At other times we should respond but do not, or we respond but do the wrong thing. Through cultivation we learn that these vexations arise from lack of mindfulness; we discover how suffering arises in us and how we cause suffering to others. Once we recognize this, we can begin to rectify our mistakes.

By all means, this is not easy. As we engage the practice, we will inevitably discover vexations and negativities in ourselves. When we fail, we should just resume practicing mindfully. We must do it again and again. Even in the simplified space of a meditation retreat, where silence is the rule, we can still be mindful in our thoughts as we go about our daily activities. We should be very clear about how we respond to situations. After retreat, when we can talk again, we need to be very aware of what we want to say and what we are saying; we will see that a clear mind and composure are essential when interacting with people. Being on retreat is a chance to begin this practice.

Buddhists should train to rectify their errors of body, speech, and mind; they should know their intentions—whether their mind is stable and clear or full of negative thoughts. A good practitioner is very clear about what actions and words are appropriate. If we do not even know our own mind, if we cannot clarify and stabilize it and thus continue causing harm with our actions and speech, enlightenment will be very remote. We need to cultivate a holistic way of being that involves mind, body, and speech, especially the mind. That is why we need to use a method of practice. A practitioner should stay on top of the method anytime, anywhere, in any situation, practicing constantly. In doing this we can purify body, speech, and mind, thus departing from negativity and error. Once we can practice with composure, we have a chance to become enlightened.

When Will You Have Another Opportunity?

In his discourse, *Impetus to Pass through the Chan Gate*, Master Huanglong Wuxin (1044–1115) asks:

> If you do not deliver this present human body in this lifetime, then, in what lifetime will you have a chance to deliver this human body?

"To deliver this present human body" is a Chan way of saying to be free from samsara, the cyclic existence of rebirth. For modern practitioners, it can be interpreted simply as to be free from suffering. You don't have to be enlightened in order to be free from suffering; you need only to be on the path to liberation. It is like taking a ferry from the shore of suffering to reach the other shore of liberation; as long as you board the ferry and begin the journey, you are on your way to liberation. Thus, "to be free" can be understood as a process of being ferried to the other shore, and the vessel we use is none other than the *Buddhadharma. It is only because we have attained this precious human form that we are able to get on this ferry. Since we have obtained a body and since we have heard the Buddhadharma, we should use this rare opportunity to practice. Think of deliverance as the process of overcoming birth and death. There is a Chan saying that to transcend birth and death is to realize complete enlightenment. The saying encourages practitioners to set a period of time to obtain this realization, whether that is a lifetime or a fixed period, such as a seven-day retreat.

Becoming enlightened is neither simple nor difficult. But in order to personally experience it, we must have the correct view of impermanence. Each moment is transient and cannot be held on to. If you cannot use this fleeting moment to practice, then you are wasting your time; if you can use it to practice, then each moment becomes precious. Cherish each moment to understand the fleeting nature of your own thoughts. Experience two kinds of impermanence of your mind: the impermanence of the thoughts that endlessly pass through it, and the impermanence of the mind itself. You must experience this for yourself; having a correct view of impermanence is the safest and most beneficial way to practice Buddhadharma.

Human life is characterized by impermanence. Even if you live to a hundred and twenty, life is still fleeting. The number of breaths you take in a lifetime may be millions, but that is still finite. If you fully understand impermanence, then you should make use of every breath you take. Then, with every inhalation and exhalation, you would be freeing this human form. This is a sure way to cross the sea of suffering to the other shore of liberation.

That does not mean you should be hasty and anxious in engaging the practice. This is like rushing to get to the ferry early but forgetting your boarding papers; everyone else boards, and you are left behind. Understand impermanence, but don't be too hasty or too anxious. Just patiently stay with the method from moment to moment. When you do this, you will realize that you are already on the ship. This is the best way to practice. Otherwise you will keep losing the practice, like getting on the boat safely and then throwing yourself overboard. Get on, and patiently stay on until you reach the other shore.

So beginning now, fully experience impermanence. Thought after thought, be completely with your practice. Put heart and mind into the method. Offer this precious life to the Buddhadharma. Practice like this and your effort will not be in vain. Knowing you have this treasure, it would be a pity to waste it day after day, moment after moment. This precious gold is originally yours, so spend it on the practice. If you do this, you will be on your way to freeing your human form.

Faith in Mind

Faith in Mind is a famous Chan poem that is attributed to the master Sengcan (d. 606), the third patriarch of Chan. It opens with the following lines:

> The supreme way is not difficult
> If only you do not pick and choose.

In these lines, Sengcan says that the path toward buddhahood is achievable if you put aside all doubts and you truly believe you can accomplish it. Thus, the first requirement for a practitioner is to have faith. Faith in what? Faith in one's own mind. "The supreme way," is the *Mahayana path of a *bodhisattva who defers self-liberation in order to help sentient beings. "If only you do not pick and choose" refers to the grave mistake of those who withhold faith in the Dharma until they can resolve all their doubts through thinking and analysis. With this kind of "picking and choosing," it is very difficult to gain a genuine entry to the practice. True entry cannot be gained by intellectual understanding but through confidence in the path and believing in one's own buddha-nature. After one engages in practice, understanding will come.

While some people lack faith, others believe that having buddha-nature means that one is already a buddha. This is another grave mistake! To see your buddha-nature is to have no more uncertainty in your mind, but that is not the same as attaining buddhahood. In the beginning, however, we must have resolute faith in our own potential to reach buddhahood. How can we give rise to such faith? The *Parinirvana *Sutra, which was spoken by the Buddha before his death, clearly states that sentient beings are endowed with buddha-nature. Similarly, the Avatamsaka Sutra states that all sentient beings are fully endowed with the "merit and virtue of a buddha"; in other words, they have buddha-nature.

The Dharma that was spoken by the Buddha arose from his own experiences and awakening, and it was transmitted and recorded as spoken words. It has been testified to by his immediate disciples, as well as by the lineage masters throughout the ages; they also had faith; they engaged in practice; they fully experienced the Dharma and transmitted it to us. So, having faith in the Buddha's Dharma, in the teachings of the Chan masters and other enlightened beings all point to one thing: believing that we have buddha-nature. Having this faith, we can practice Chan well.

In the *Agamas and the *Nikayas, the collected early discourses of the Buddha, practice is defined as consisting of four disciplines, or studies, the first of which is faith. Faith is the foundation of the other three studies of precepts, meditation, and wisdom. Without faith one cannot truly begin to practice the so-called higher studies, but with faith they can advance stage by stage, progressing on the path. Without faith, studying precepts, meditation, and wisdom would be in vain. Later sutras, like the Avatamsaka, clearly state that faith is the foundation of the path and is the mother of virtue and merit.

Resolute faith is not easy to come by, and it is also difficult to maintain. Those with sharp karmic roots can quickly give rise to faith when they encounter the Dharma; they will have confidence in the path; having heard the teachings on enlightenment and buddha-nature, they will engage in practice. Having faith, they are diligent, steady, and do not regress. Theirs is the fruit of merit and virtue accumulated over past lives, resulting in good karmic disposition in the current life.

Others can begin with the same faith but eventually regress in confidence; they engage the practice, but due to karmic obstacles, they go astray. If they meet favorable conditions later, they might return to practice, and they can go back and forth like this. Their karmic dispositions are not so firm and not so deep. To practice to good effect we must give rise to faith, be constantly diligent, and trust in the path. When our practice is erratic, we are at best planting good karma, not realizing the path. While it is normal for sentient beings to advance and regress, we should always strive to give rise to faith. Ashvaghosha's (80–150?) treatise, *The Awakening of Mahayana Faith*, speaks of the ten levels of faith. When one's faith has progressed through the ten levels and has fully ripened, then they will not regress.

That it is rare to attain a human form is good reason to use this precious life to practice. We can accept the idea that to hear the Dharma is rare, but for some it is hard to accept that it is rare to obtain a human birth. In the scriptures the Buddha said that to obtain human form was rare and precious, and in all his wisdom and omniscience, the Buddha surely would not deceive us. One thing is certain: life is impermanent and fleeting. Gold and diamonds can be replaced, but once this life fades into the past, it cannot be replaced. Therefore, life is precious; each moment is precious; every breath is precious. A retreat is just a few days in your life, but it too is precious. Use it well to engage your practice and to investigate your huatou.

Light and Sound Outside the Gate

Master Dahui Zonggao could be at times critical of people who read the works of the masters and think they have gotten Chan. In fact, at the moment of death, when facing King Yama, such people will find that all their reading was of little use. Intellectually inclined practitioners are also prone to want quick results. But the insights they derive from texts are shallow and do not yield true benefits. In Chan, we say that these practitioners are "walking on air," not grounded in actual practice. Because their feet are not firmly planted, they easily stumble. Rather than taking shortcuts, it is better to practice with solid, enduring effort, each step firmly on the ground, moving forward with earnestness and sincerity. Some people who think they are very sharp can accomplish in one day what might take others ten. At least that is what they believe. Of course there are those rare people who can do this and actually gain real benefits. However, usually such people have had deep practice in previous lives, allowing them to pick up things very quickly.

In seeking quick results, one can gain insights that are likely shallow and short-lived, dissipating like flashes of light. For the moment their mind is clear and without vexations, but if there is still self-attachment, the experience is shallow and of little use. More seriously, practicing with a seeking mind can attract demonic influences. A practitioner who seeks a quick path to buddhahood can interpret any altered state as attaining awakening or supernatural ability. In fact, since time immemorial people have believed they are incarnated buddhas. That belief is not uncommon even today. This is indeed dangerous if they mislead others.

To avoid the pitfalls of shallow attainment and demonic influence, be solidly grounded in practice. Even though huatou should be practiced without effort, you need to ground it with endurance and patience, knowing that you only get out of it what you put into it. At the same time, you should practice without anticipating results. You may think that a ten-day retreat is a test of endurance, but compared to a lifetime of practice, it is nothing. So, whether you vow to attend retreat or to practice for a whole lifetime, proceed with a patient and enduring mind: this is more likely to reap genuinely worthwhile results.

Master Xuyun had a disciple who followed him for many years, working in the fields, building monasteries, and traveling with him to other temples. One day, the monk asked Xuyun to give him some Dharma teachings. Xuyun told the monk that after all these years he had no Dharma to teach, and besides, there was really no need to hear the Dharma. He told the monk that by using his huatou, he could find the Dharma within himself. Touched by these words, the monk prostrated to Xuyun and remained with him. We don't know if this monk became enlightened, but we do know that practicing under the same master for a long time helps to build a solid foundation. Likewise, the purpose of retreat is to habituate yourself to practice so that you can use it in daily life. If you don't practice in daily life but come to retreat and call that practice, getting good results will be hard. What is more beneficial is to practice in daily life and then come on retreat to rekindle and deepen your practice. In fact, in the history of Chan, there have been many practitioners who got enlightened outside of the meditation hall.

From a conventional view, it is normal, for example, to get an education with the goal of becoming a professor. But from the Chan point of view, it is contrary to start with the goal of becoming a Chan master, because that indicates a strong self-center. Starting with such a goal, it would be possible to use the huatou method as a path to enlightenment, but even if one had some kind of awakening, it would not be genuine. We call that kind of experience "light and sound outside the gate." Being a Chan master requires more

than an experience of emptiness; it also requires skillful means—
the necessary social as well as teaching skills. It is more than just
being free from vexations.

Is it true that enlightened persons do not have any vexations?
Enlightenment can be shallow, or it can be deep. A shallow enlightenment means that, at a minimum, that person has gained an insight
into the nature of phenomena and self as empty. For such people
vexations still exist, but they are immediately clear about it when they
have vexations. For such a person practice is still necessary. People
who are deeply and thoroughly enlightened do not experience vexations within themselves, but that is not to say that they are completely
without vexations. In other words, they may carry residual tendencies
from past lifetimes that are perceived by others as vexations. Even
though they exist as residues and cause no new vexations for that
person, their actions may still have effects on others. While such a
person is clear that they have no inner vexations, they are aware of
these habitual tendencies and therefore still feel the need to practice.

Do thoroughly enlightened people still feel happiness, anger,
sadness, joy, and so on? We all know about these kinds of emotions. For people who are swayed by circumstances and the whims
of the environment, these are the typical contents of their minds.
Enlightened people also have such emotions, but they are natural responses as methods to help others. If responding to people
requires feelings appropriate to the circumstance, such emotions
will manifest even in enlightened people. However, their minds
are not colored by these emotions. It is not that they are inca-
pable of responding to others, but their minds are unwavering in
responding, forever at rest. So, when an enlightened person shows
happiness, people may perceive them as happy, but the enlightened person's mind is not moving. When an enlightened person
manifests anger, it is because the circumstance calls for it, but the
content of their mind is not anger, hatred, resentment, and so on.
So with sadness and joy—these feelings manifest according to the

circumstances, but the minds of the enlightened do not have the coloration of these emotions. Such is the mental state of someone who is deeply enlightened.

Those who are not yet enlightened can still practice huatou to reduce the influence of strong emotions. If practicing huatou can help you avoid being enraptured by your vexations, you will lessen the harm you cause. You may not think of happiness and joy as vexations, but they are because they stem from grasping and self-attachment. As such they are neither wisdom nor compassion. When you respond to the world with neither wisdom nor compassion but rather with your emotions, you may end up hurting more than helping. Because of this, we should use huatou in daily life.

Do enlightened practitioners still need to practice? They certainly do. Master Xuyun practiced huatou both before and after enlightenment. The Chan patriarchs and lineage masters practiced all their lives and continued even after great awakening. It is like eating and brushing your teeth—it is something you do every day. It is the same with enlightenment; practice continues in long and enduring ways. In the sutras we read of great bodhisattvas, awakened beings, who have practiced for many *kalpas* since time without beginning. The reality is that practice continues even after one is enlightened. If you see yourself as a longtime practitioner in this life, that is nothing compared to even one kalpa. You may think, "You know, that is longer than I expected, maybe longer than I am willing to endure." If you have ideas like these, you should quickly get rid of them. Therefore, be patient, have an enduring mind, and just use the method.

Upholding the Precepts

Upholding the precepts is not just for monastics but for laypeople as well. To live in society one must behave in accordance with certain standards that support an ethical way of life. In Buddhism these standards are called "precepts." Therefore, the first requirement for Buddhists is to not only live ethically for oneself but also for the sake of others. Without ethical standards we hurt ourselves just as if we dropped a big rock on our own foot. We would also have trouble relating to other people. So, to speak about enlightenment is very remote if we cannot first live an ethical way of life.

Some people naively think that it is fine to have vexations that will all be resolved when they become enlightened. This naive idea implies that it is all right to live unethically while seeking enlightenment. Some also believe that after they get enlightened, they are free to do whatever they want. If enlightened people were above the precepts and lived without restraint, then some of them would end up in jail. Both of these are upside-down views.

At the end of every retreat we transmit the *Five Precepts to those who are willing to accept them and undergo the ceremony of *taking refuge. Receiving and keeping the precepts is not that difficult because they constitute the very basic standards for living in society. Moreover, they help reduce our vexations to the minimum as well as harmonizing our relations with others. Far from being too restraining, they actually protect us from harm like a suit of armor.

The precepts are also aids to meditative concentration. Through being mindful of our conduct, we are free from the harmful consequences of breaking the precepts, thus allowing our mind to be calm and collected. Someone who does not uphold the precepts will have a chaotic mind, and it will be very difficult to settle down when they come to retreat. Once they begin meditating, they will think about this and that, day after day. Ultimately, practice for them becomes very difficult. Therefore, we can say that upholding the precepts is an expedient means for cultivating *samadhi, or "meditative concentration." In a retreat, you will notice how settled and clear your mind can get. That is because daily living in a retreat is regulated to provide no opportunity for trouble and agitation. So, the whole retreat environment is conducive to naturally upholding the precepts. Because there is no social engagement, this means we should be always mindful and in touch with the practice. So, we can see that retreat life embodies the principle of a regulated and stable environment. This is the key for ethical living.

As I said, precepts are expedient means to attain samadhi. Prior to being able to cultivate samadhi, the mind is typically chaotic, unsettled, floating, and aimless. In order to reach a concentrated state, we must train ourselves to bring this scattered mind to single-mindedness. This happens when the mind is able to settle on just one thought from one instant to the next. This "one thought" is a metaphor for staying with your huatou, or any other method, so that from moment to moment, the mind does not scatter or stray off the practice. This single-mindedness is a prerequisite for entering samadhi. When you can do this, after some time of staying on a single thought—like links in a continuous chain—your mind will abide in a state we can call "samadhi."

This samadhi can be shallow, or it can be deep. At a shallow level this is simply a somewhat deeper level of single-mindedness where the previous and following thoughts are of the same content—there is the practice and nothing else. At a deep level the mind abides in a vast spaciousness without any conscious thinking. So the difference is one of the mind staying on one thought and the mind having no thoughts at all.

Diligence and Humility

In a race, the last lap is the most important one—you want to make a strong finish, you don't want to stumble, and you don't want to give up before crossing the finish line. Similarly, on a retreat you also want to make a strong finish and not stumble by giving in to deluded thoughts and emotional ups and downs. And of course, you don't want to give up before the retreat is over. However, the analogy is not perfect. In the beginning of a race the runners are

41

conserving their energy, while on the last lap they are putting forth their utmost effort. Conversely, on a Chan retreat the most energy is required in the beginning, but later on your body adjusts to Chan life and your mind becomes attuned to the practice method. There's a Chan saying, "On the first three days of a 'Chan seven,' each day is like a year; the next three days are like riding a fast horse, and the last day is a puff of smoke." What this says is that at the end, a retreat seems to have gone so fast you don't even see its shadow. However, because your body and mind have adjusted, there is a temptation to take it easy in the last days of retreat. One may even think, "Well, since I haven't gotten enlightened, I may as well relax." Or, "I won't gain anything more, so I'll just hang around and tomorrow I will be going home." If you think like this, it will be most pitiable, and coming to retreat will have really been a waste.

On retreat, we develop a habit of diligence so that when we return to daily life, it will serve us well. However much we can be diligent while we are here, that much will we benefit if we are diligent at home. If we cannot be diligent here where all the conditions are right, how can we be diligent at home?

Humility can be understood from two points of view. First, there is the humility that comes when we recognize that we often create vexations for ourselves as well as for others; we bring suffering to others while perpetuating our own negativity. The second aspect of humility refers to those things we could have done better at but have not; we feel shame for not doing better. From these two standpoints, we then reflect on why we should feel humble.

Those without shame or humility will continue to create vexations and negativities for themselves and others. They shun their responsibilities while seeking benefits for themselves. If we are humble, our thoughts, actions, and speech can become purer; otherwise we continue to be mired in vexation. Humility also gives rise to other virtues such as faith and confidence. This makes it easier to generate the aspiration to enlightenment and to nourish renunciation. Therefore, diligence and humility go hand in hand in the practice of the bodhisattva way of life, the way of wisdom and compassion.

It is because we lack humility that we have vexations, and it is because we have no shame that we shun responsibility. When we lack humility, we will have conflicts within ourselves and we will inflict suffering on others. If we are humble, we recognize our own vexations and we know when we stray off the Dharma path. When we vex others, we know we have strayed from compassion. Without humility we cannot recognize our shortcomings or our inability to practice Dharma. Therefore humility is very much related to not harming oneself or others. It is wisdom if you can avoid internal conflicts, and it is compassion when you can avoid hurting others. So, wisdom, compassion, and humility—the three are all related.

When we act humbly, other people may see us as weak and try to take advantage. Or, if we do not fulfill their needs, they may accuse us of lacking compassion. "How can you consider yourself a Buddhist?" In such cases we should use wisdom to not give them an opportunity to create bad karma, and we should not create any bad karma ourselves. So, we respond appropriately with wisdom and with compassion. If we cannot help such a person, we should be ashamed that we lack the wisdom to respond appropriately.

Repentance

Many people think humility is a feeling of inferiority or low self-esteem. They think that being humble means one is worthless. This is not a correct understanding. On the contrary, from a genuine feeling of humility, self-confidence can be established. This self-confidence comes from the recognition of what one truly is. Thus, being humble, one can be more diligent in correcting and in improving themselves. Furthermore, a sense of inferiority can lead to a flightiness and instability, whereas humility grounds oneself in a true perspective—one recognizes and understands their mistakes and shortcomings; their character becomes more stable, down-to-earth, with an air of solidity. In Chinese terms, you could say that one's chi flows subtly downward as opposed to an insecure person, whose chi is floating and unsettled.

Closely related to humility is repentance. People misunderstand repentance as being regret or resentment. For example, we aspire to something, but due to causes and conditions we do not succeed; not only that, we may even suffer a loss or setback. As a result we may feel regret or resentment, but this is not really repentance. If things do not turn out the way we want, it is due to causes and conditions, and there is no need to be regretful or resentful. Because the outcome is not what we expected, we may decide out of resentment never to try again. The act itself was purposeful; it just turned out in an unexpected way. This is not to say that we should give up trying or that we should regret having done it. If food gets caught in your throat, it would be foolish to say, "I'll never eat again." On the other hand if we do something wrong or something that turns out not as expected, we should think about how we can do better next time. This is the true meaning of repentance—thinking through, introspecting, and analyzing to find ways we can make corrections and improve. The true meaning of repentance is recognizing and correcting mistakes and shortcomings, not feeling bad about what happened in the past.

Repentance goes beyond recognizing our misdeeds, because often we do not know or remember our misdeeds. We can't remember everything we have ever done, but we should still repent for anything that might have caused harm. We have lived through countless cycles of birth and death, and in each life we have probably done negative things that leave karmic imprints on our psyche. This karmic consciousness contains the seeds or potential for future retribution. If we cannot recall everything we have done in this life, how much harder would it be to recall our lives from aeons ago? All our past actions have karmic repercussions in our present as well as future lives. When causes and conditions ripen, we then receive retribution. We should therefore accept the responsibility for all our actions throughout our many lives and repent for them. Through repentance we change our behavior, thus avoiding planting new seeds for negative karma. So long as we maintain humility and a repentant mind, whatever seeds we sow are less likely to manifest as heavy retribution.

Another reason we are unable to recognize our shortcomings and mistakes is because we lack wisdom; our ignorance blinds us to insight into our conduct. Often, we cannot tell what is right and what is wrong, and due to ignorance we cause harm even when we mean to be righteous. Even when someone points out our misdeeds, we still hold on to our misguided view. So, lacking wisdom, we cannot recognize our faults and we continue to act against our good intentions. Something that we think is right may not be appropriate for other people, and yet we try to impose our ways on others. The fact that our shoes fit comfortably does not necessarily mean they are right for someone else.

We also find it difficult to repent when we make alibis or blame others in order to save face. Thus, we persist in deceiving ourselves and others to avoid accepting responsibility. This self-deception creates inner conflicts that increase vexations and decrease wisdom. As a result we will encounter obstacles in our dealings with others. Some of these obstacles will be visible; others not so visible. Nevertheless, in our past we have created opposition to others or incurred karmic debts, and no matter how hard we may try to avoid it, retribution will find us. Our conscience tells us that we have indeed done negative things and, because of this, karmic retribution will follow. Therefore, we should diligently repent to prevent the arising of causes and conditions that will cause karmic seeds to ripen. Without repentance, all sorts of seen or unseen obstacles arising internally or from the outside will continue to manifest.

To repent does not mean trying to escape our karma; to repent is to recognize that we have done negative things and created negative karma, but we are vowing to change. Being repentant is analogous to being mindful that, although we owe people money, we are not trying to escape repaying them. If we approached our creditors and made a vow to repay our debts, they might allow us more time to repay. This is somewhat like alleviating our karma by repenting. Because we have confronted the reality of our bad karma, we can change our behavior so that we create less karma for future retribution. With diligent practice we can acquire some wisdom and skillful means and not only repay our karmic debts, but repay with interest by helping others. When we repent, obstacles can be transformed into favorable conditions for practice. To continue the analogy, because we are sincere, our creditors may see we are trustworthy and negotiate better terms. In terms of repentance, giving rise to humility can help us overcome obstacles to practice, and when we attain some wisdom, we are in a better position to help others.

Sometimes someone whom you have offended only wants justice, and if you refuse to recognize your error, this makes matters worse. They will come after you even more: "Do you know what you did to me?" And you say, "No, I did not do anything wrong." At some point they may come after you with even more anger just to prove you wrong and get their justice. But if you showed some repentance, the situation could change for the better.

Once, I observed a man who was in a great rush. He was holding several bags, and as he ran through this crowded place, his bags were bumping into people. He hit one particular man very hard but just kept going. That fellow who was hit ran up to him and grabbed him: "You bumped into me and did not even apologize!" The man with the bags replied, "I didn't run into you. Get out of my way, I'm in a rush." The man who was hit was furious: "Not only did you not apologize for running into me, you're denying it."

Previously, the man with the bags was in a rush to get somewhere. Now, because he was unable to admit his fault, he was wasting time arguing. Witnessing all this, I went up to both of them and said, "I saw you hit the man with the bag, but it was unintentional." The man with the bags turned around and said, "You, who are you? Just because you say I hit him with the bag, it doesn't mean I really did it."

Calmly, I replied, "First of all, you obviously want to get somewhere very quickly, and yet you run into people, do not admit your mistake, and now you're stuck here wasting time. So, all you have to do is apologize sincerely and everything will be over." And the man sighed, "OK. This is my unlucky day. I'm sorry," and because he said it in such a self-pitying tone, the man who got run into said, "*Your* unlucky day? *My* unlucky day!" And they started quarreling again, and I continued being the middleman: "If you said with sincerity, 'I apologize. I was in a hurry. Are you OK? Is there any other thing you would like me to do?' then you could be on your way."

The man with the bags replied, "I'm not going to say that." I said, "If you're not going to say that, then, as things go on like this, you'll end up in the police station. And just to assure you, I will be the witness." [*Laughter*] And he said, "You can't do that. You're a monk." And I said, "Yes, monks do good deeds like this." [*Laughter*] And then he said, "OK, OK, fine. I apologize. Please forgive me." And he added, "Have pity on me. I'm in a hurry, and I hope everything is fine with you. Please let me go, I beg you. I have to go now." So the man just let this fellow go. And after he left, I said to the man that got run into, "Well, you see this day as your unlucky day, but maybe you can learn a lesson from it."

The point of this story is that repentance can alleviate suffering because we recognize our mistakes and aspire to change, and because of this attitude, we can alleviate karma. The other person may only be looking for justice; and once we can recognize our mistakes, they may forgive us.

Confidence, Determination, and Long-Enduring Mind

As Buddhists, we believe that when we are fortunate enough to acquire a body, we should use it to engage in practice. Nonpractitioners also come into the world with a body, but oftentimes they use it to create negative karma. Such a person is pitiable, because his life has no meaning; he follows the whims of the environment, and wallows in circumstances. Like a boat adrift on the ocean, wherever the current flows, the boat follows. But to a practitioner, life has a profound meaning that comes from making full use of the body and mind to engage in practice. For such a person the goal is quite clear.

A skillful sailor knows the ocean currents, is able to map out a destination, and has a clear idea where the boat is heading. He also knows the potential dangers that lie ahead and how to respond to them. Likewise, a huatou practitioner knows the goal, the direction, and the skills required to navigate through the sea of life. Without a doubt, our destination is enlightenment. However, the practitioner must skillfully use the method, know when to advance or retreat, when to press on, and when to rest. It is like navigating—when there are turbulent waves, the sailor knows how to deal with it. If he can't find a safe harbor, then certainly he must acquire the skill to endure the waves. Likewise, a huatou practitioner will respond to difficulties properly and with precision. If he encounters great difficulties, he will know how to take the backward step and use skillful means to overcome the obstacle. So if he guides his life with the principles of the huatou method, even though he may not reach enlightenment in this lifetime, he will live a very harmonious, peaceful life full of meaning.

With regards to the practice of huatou, the main one we should engage in is either "Wu?" or "What is wu?" The reason is because this wu is extremely powerful for enduring, lifelong practice. The mind is stunned by just asking "Wu?" whose literal meaning is "nothing" or "nonexistent." So if we ask about "nothing," where can the mind turn? On the other hand, if we use a huatou like "Who am I?"

the self-referential nature of this question allows too much room for ideation. "*Wu,*" because of its simplicity and opaqueness, does not allow room for conceptualization, and that is where its power lies.

As I said earlier, Dahui Zonggao had a view of huatou in which he taught that one reserves power in order to gain power. His teaching focuses on engaging huatou in the midst of adversity as the most opportune time to bring forth one's huatou, investigate it, and gain an entry. Conventional meditation practice emphasizes preparation and regulated conditions for sitting. Dahui's students were already grounded in the basics of practice, so he swept away these preparatory concerns and asked them to focus on those times when we don't have such favorable conditions. He taught that when you encounter adversity, you can turn it into an opportunity to practice. It is the ability to immediately use whatever situation you face to gain power in the practice.

To practice huatou well, you must have conviction as well as determination, and you must make the path enduring. Actually, conviction, determination, and long-enduring mind are crucial for practice in general. Without confidence, right from the start you will find huatou boring. Without determination, minor difficulties will test your resolve. Without long-enduring mind, after ten days of retreat, will your practice also end? Then you wait until the next retreat to rekindle your practice. If you always have to rekindle your practice, the flame will not burn with consistency, and it will lack power. Only when you have an enduring mind will you be able to bring the practice into your daily life. If you maintain momentum between retreats, next time you will advance more quickly. So the three keys to practice are confidence, determination, and a long-enduring mind.

In the midst of the practice you will sometimes experience reactions. Sometimes they will be pleasant, sometimes discomforting. At times you will experience illusions that spring either from your imagination or from sights and sounds around you. These experiences are, generally speaking, normal. However it is crucial to not get caught up in them. Simply accept them for what they are without attaching or rejecting them and without labeling them "good" or "bad." Do not dwell on them nor add your own ideas. Simply see them for what they are, neither good nor bad, and persist in your method. That is the correct attitude toward meditation experiences.

In the course of practice, you may also encounter fear and anticipation: you fear the unknown, or you anticipate awakening. Please ignore these feelings, because they lead away from making progress. If you harbor these attitudes, it is possible for so-called demonic states, or delusions, to take hold of you. Among these delusions are ideas that you have attained enlightenment or have gained supernatural powers. So do not engage in fear or anticipation, as they are obstructions.

What is enlightenment? It is the manifestation of wisdom. Not worldly wisdom but the wisdom of *prajna*—a mind free from fear, from expectation, from the attitudes and thoughts that stem from self-centeredness. Prajna is letting go of the myriad faces and attitudes that arise from a view in which the world revolves around us. Prajna is the disappearance of self-attachment; it is the mind of enlightenment.

When you are in perfect accordance with wisdom, you will experience enlightenment, and compassion will accompany it. This is not something sought after but a natural course of events. This compassion is a natural response to sentient beings—you will want to benefit others. However, if you seek enlightenment, neither wisdom nor compassion will happen because you are moving contrary to the natural course. I myself have not experienced great enlightenment, but I have experienced a little bit of wisdom. However, whatever wisdom and compassion I have realized comes from confidence, determination, and a long-enduring mind.

THE MIDDLE WAY

Practice and the Middle Way

HOW DOES THE METHOD OF HUATOU relate to the Buddhadharma? In fact, they are inseparable. The Buddhadharma encompasses Chan. If Chan is devoid of Buddhadharma, it would not be correct Chan. When we practice huatou, we also practice Buddhadharma and vice versa. I will explain what this means.

As a young prince, Shakyamuni witnessed sickness, suffering, and death, and left home in order to find a way out of suffering. Before he became the Buddha, he went through years of hardship, cultivating spiritual disciplines, practicing different methods of meditation, learning from various teachers. While all this helped Shakyamuni to develop spiritually, it was not ultimately satisfying because he still could not find a way to relieve human suffering. He eventually set out on his own, practicing asceticism for six years. After this period of extreme self-denial and physical pain, he was weak and exhausted, and he still had not realized his goal. He began to realize that extreme asceticism was adding suffering to suffering. Having already left behind a princely life and having failed to attain his goal through asceticism, Shakyamuni decided that he must find a way between the two extremes.

Thus he discovered the *Middle Way, resting when he was tired and eating when he was hungry. To regain his strength, he once accepted an offering of goat's milk from a young woman. When he was healthy again, he found a tree under which he could meditate. He vowed to sit in meditation until he attained enlightenment. Letting go of all his previous experiences and ideas, on the sixth night he saw the morning star shining brilliantly. At that moment, he suddenly awakened to buddhahood and became the Buddha. What he experienced was a sudden enlightenment that can only come when one lets go of every attachment. Some people may look at the stars and think, "How beautiful! No wonder Shakyamuni became enlightened." But you can look at stars until your dying day and still not become enlightened. The real cause of his enlightenment was being able to let go of everything in his mind.

If through practicing huatou you can give rise to the doubt sensation, and if that becomes a great doubt mass enveloping your whole being, then even a bird shitting on your head can bring on enlightenment. Those droppings would not be the cause of your enlightenment but just one of the causes and conditions, a catalyst if you will, that brings about enlightenment. If and when enlightenment comes to you, it will be out of the ripening of your own mind-ground. When this mind-ground is sufficiently ripened by causes and conditions, any event can be a stimulus for it to cast off the illusory self. When the thinking mind drops away like that, one may realize sudden enlightenment.

Shakyamuni Buddha realized that asceticism could not bring enlightenment if the sense of self was still solid after enduring all that hardship, particularly a self that was attached to attaining enlightenment. At the very least, however, asceticism restrains the body, mind, and speech, so that one does not engage in negative acts. If Shakyamuni had given up asceticism for hedonism, then enlightenment would have been even more distant. If he had indulged in the five sense desires, that would not be considered practice. At least being ascetic can help one become aware of vexations, while drowning oneself in pleasures can make one blind to vexation, even while being surrounded by it. Shakyamuni then decided to tread the middle path, avoiding the extremes of asceticism and hedonism.

Many people think that the Middle Way means neither indulging in hedonism nor enduring suffering, but that is a mistake if it means doing nothing. The Middle Way that the Dharma speaks of is the underlying truth that all existence consists of the dynamic workings of causes and conditions. The workings of causes and conditions testify that there is no inherent, independent, self-existing entity that we can call an "I" or a "self." Through causes and conditions, things manifest in a fluid, dynamic way, constantly changing. Thus, all things are impermanent, coming together because of the aggregation of various causes and conditions, and we call this "conditioned existence." In order to come into being, all things depend on other things happening. Things also perish because of causes and conditions. This truth of coming into being and perishing can be applied to everything. If we were to characterize phenomena as having self-nature, then we would call that nature "emptiness." This emptiness is not a void; rather, its nature is that of an aggregation of conditions that are themselves impermanent and empty. By another name, this emptiness is called "buddha-nature." This buddha-nature is in direct opposition to self-centeredness— the idea that within us somewhere is a permanent self, an "I" that governs all of our actions of body, speech, and thought. When we take a closer look at what we call this "I," we discover that it, too, is an aggregate of causes and conditions. The "self" is actually a nexus of mental defilements and vexations—thoughts, emotions, feelings, ideas, memories—transforming, ever-changing, fluid, and dynamic. When someone directly perceives that there is no enduring reality in the phenomenon of self, that is to say—that the self is empty—this is the realization of buddha-nature.

The Middle Way of Buddhism means not attaching to extremes and not clinging to the middle either. Essentially, practicing the Middle Way means not attaching to the sense of self and not attaching to what belongs to the self. If we can do this with the aid of huatou practice, then we will be practicing in accordance with the Middle Way of the Buddha.

Huatou and the Middle Way

How do we realize this buddha-nature? By letting go of attachments and letting go of the inner as well as the outer self. The inner self refers to the "I," while the outer self refers to everything we consider as "mine." By letting go of both the inner and outer self, we awaken to the Middle Way. But how does the practice of huatou relate to this Middle Way? Our sense of self is the identity we create with our thinking mind, our views, and our thoughts. The huatou is a tool that we can use to peel away the numerous layers of the self. So, in the process of investigating the huatou, the self will manifest as various answers to the huatou. Peeling away the layers of self is actually getting rid of the wandering thoughts, delusions, and attachments that arise in meditation. If we can free the mind from all these defilements, it will experience a state we call "genuine emptiness," or buddha-nature.

At a more subtle level, as we go deeper into our meditation, thoughts from the inner psyche will manifest or may arise from our store of acquired knowledge. For example, while working on "What is *wu*?" an answer like "*true suchness" can come up, seemingly out of nowhere. Because it is sudden and abrupt, we may take that as the answer to our huatou; we may seriously think we have experienced emptiness. When something like this happens, it is another manifestation of self, a deluded thought that we should put down.

What do I mean by putting down deluded thoughts? We must realize that originally there are no deluded thoughts in the mind, so wandering thoughts themselves lack a fixed, enduring nature. What we call the self is merely the ongoing succession of delusions, one after another. If we can sever this chain, the self will also vanish. Therefore, the process begins with peeling away the layers of deluded thinking. We do that by single-mindedly holding on to our huatou, never giving delusion the opportunity to arise. If we persist, gradually deluded thoughts will subside. This is not to say they will no longer exist, but that they are just not active. If you can do this for a sustained period, we call that "samadhi"—a temporary silencing of wandering thoughts. However, that is not sufficient, because wandering thoughts can rise again and the sense of self will resume.

Besides being single-minded in practicing huatou, we must generate the doubt sensation. Once we give rise to the doubt sensation, we are truly investigating huatou. With wholehearted and single-minded effort, the doubt sensation can evolve into a great doubt mass that engulfs our whole being. When we continue the urgent questioning, when wandering thoughts no longer surface, when no deluded thinking arises, and when causes and conditions are ripe, the great doubt mass will ultimately shatter and sweep away all deluded thinking, breaking the chain of wandering thoughts. And since the self is merely a chain of wandering thoughts, at that moment the self will be completely cast off.

Fundamental Ignorance

The Buddha said that the reason we are unable to end suffering is due to fundamental ignorance. Out of this nexus of fundamental ignorance, our actions create afflictions and sustain our vexations, all of which leads to karmic retribution. Since we have planted the causes, the inevitable results will follow. As a result we remain in the cycle of birth and death. To liberate ourselves from this cycle, we must uproot the fundamental ignorance that causes us to create karma. When the cause of karma ceases, we will no longer receive the retribution of birth and death.

Simply put, fundamental ignorance consists of all the erroneous views that we hold about ourselves and the world. In Buddhism we also call them "upside-down" or "inverted" views. When we hold these upside-down views, we do harmful things and we ultimately receive due retribution as suffering. One aspect of this fundamental ignorance is that the world is impermanent with everything in constant flux, yet people hold on to things as if they were permanent. People base their sense of security on fleeting things, and ultimately find themselves grasping at nothing, because all things change constantly and do not last. So, when people build their security and expectations on impermanent things, eventually they will lose hope and end up with nothing.

Things change because causes collaborating with conditions results in the appearance of phenomena, and since other causes and conditions are at play, these phenomena change in the course of time. Eventually, again due to causes and conditions, the phenomena will perish. In other words, things exist because of causes and conditions, and they also perish because of causes and conditions. So, when people do not understand how the world operates and build their hopes and expectations on changing phenomena, pain and suffering—a death in the family, a career change, losing something cherished—ensue. The reason they experience this is because they do not see that from the very beginning, things are in a constant state of change. Reality is such that we constantly live amidst change, and it is inevitable that things which arise will in time perish.

A lady I know got divorced when her son was seven. At that time he told his mother, "If father does not want you anymore, I will take good care of you for the rest of my life." The mother was quite touched. Ten years later the boy is a teenager who constantly scolds his mother, using her divorce as a way to hurt her, saying things like, "You deserve it. It's only natural that Dad divorced you," or even worse. The mother is greatly hurt by all of this and said to me, "When he was seven, he was so kind and sensitive, and now he wants me to die. What kind of karma did I create to deserve this?"

I said to her, "This is the workings of causes and conditions in your life, so anything is possible. To avoid more pain and suffering, just focus on being a responsible mother. Do your best, and do not have any expectations of the boy, such as hoping he will be kind and take care of you. If you have such expectations, when things do not turn out well, you will suffer. The nature of the world is just the workings of many causes and conditions. All you can do is live out your life, taking care of yourself and those you are supposed to take care of."

The inability to face impermanence leads to suffering, but if we can fully accept impermanence in life, this is the beginning of liberation. Suffering results when we base our hopes on things that are transient, and the reason we do this is because of attachment to self. Collectively, all our possessions, the things we rely on, our hopes and expectations, all establish our sense of self. When we can face impermanence, our self-attachment lessens because we will not hold on so strongly to fleeting things; we do not see the self as reality confirming its own existence. Therefore, if one accepts impermanence in all situations and understands it fully, self-attachment is absent, and they realize emptiness; they become empty of vexations and attachments that result from relying on transient things. Otherwise, trying to achieve liberation is like tying oneself with rope while complaining, "I'm tied up in knots!" That is fundamental ignorance.

Why do some people have more vexations after they start practicing? The reason is because they expect to get rid of their suffering through practicing. So, along the way while practicing, they acquire more vexations. They have the same upside-down views as before, except they are now on a spiritual path. They hope for uplifting experiences, and if they get "good" results, they are quite proud and they never forget it. They are sincere and care very much about their practice; they think in terms of progress, and they are very concerned that the method that they use will lead to some supposed great result. This is like the person who is already tied up in knots making even more knots.

In Chan we speak of the diamond sword of wisdom that one uses to cut away all manner of attachments. Whatever attachment one finds within themselves, they should use this sword to sweep it away. If within one instant one is free from any kind of attachment, that is one instant of liberation. If one can do this continuously, being free from all kinds of attachment, then at all times they are liberated.

If you have the attitude of detachment in your practice, whether you experience benefits or obstacles, you will be unhindered, free, and at ease. If you experience something good, tell yourself it is fleeting and nothing to be proud of. If your practice is not going smoothly and you have wandering thoughts, that's also impermanent. There's no need to be upset. In either case you can be free and at ease. Whether you get enlightened is simply not at issue. At the very moment of detachment, you are liberated. So, you should practice with this attitude, using the principle of detachment.

Correct Views

To successfully practice Chan, you need more than just the methods of meditation; you should also have the proper attitudes: you should have faith and confidence; you should make vows; you should have a compassionate heart; and you should cultivate renunciation. There are other supporting attitudes than these four, but these are fundamental.

All religions are established on faith, and some of them encourage or even require devotees to believe in some god or a deity. In Chan your faith is primarily in yourself; you should believe that you have good karmic roots, and that you have the potential to become enlightened. If you do not have this kind of faith, you can be easily deterred as soon as you encounter obstacles and think you are not suitable for this practice. Therefore it is most important to have faith in yourself.

Secondly, you should have faith in the Dharma; you should believe that practicing Dharma will illuminate your mind and allow you to experience your true self-nature. This Dharma is nothing more than the proper concepts and methods of practice; without faith in the Dharma, you will not be able to accept it much less cultivate it. This Dharma includes the proper views, concepts, and methods of practice as transmitted by a teacher and spoken originally by the Buddha. So, to establish confidence in the Dharma, you should first have confidence in the teacher—you believe that your teacher not only understands the Dharma, but also has gained some personal realization. You should believe that the Dharma the teacher is transmitting is appropriate for you and in accordance with the teachings the Buddha expounded.

To establish genuine faith, you must use the faith that you already have in the Dharma; you must also have the correct views and you must believe in your methods of practice. Once you have used the methods and gained some direct experience, you will be more confident and be able to ascertain the meaning of Dharma in your life. When you testify to the Dharma based on your experience, then that is genuine faith.

I have said that once you have experienced your self-nature, you will not regress in the practice. This is what testifying to the Dharma means: having personally experienced emptiness, you will no longer regress in faith in yourself, in the Dharma, in the teacher, and in the Buddha. If you take an aspirin for a headache and the headache goes away, that is a personal experience you can attest to. Similarly, when you take Dharma medicine and it cures you, your faith is much more grounded.

But before you take the medicine, how can you have faith that it will work for you? There are several ways. You can recognize that you are spiritually ill and need medicine. In this analogy, the prescribed medicine is the Dharma and it is available through a teacher, so you may as well try it. Secondly, your teacher has other students who seem to have faith in him or her, so you can establish faith by inference. Since other students seem to be benefiting, perhaps you can too. So those are ways you establish faith in the beginning.

Next is making vows. Every day on retreat we recite the *Four Great Vows: we vow to deliver sentient beings, we vow to cut off vexations, we vow to master the Dharma, and we vow to accomplish buddhahood. Among these the most important is to reach buddhahood. When you make this vow, you have also generated *bodhichitta, or *bodhi-mind. But this bodhi-mind is grounded in delivering sentient beings, in cutting off vexations, and in mastering the Dharma.

Making vows gives us a sense of direction without which our path would be aimless, but when we make the Four Great Vows, we will gain clear guidance toward an ultimate goal, which is none other than supreme buddhahood. You will wonder if it is all attainable. Yes it is, but you cannot assume it is achievable in one or even many lifetimes. The Buddha entered *nirvana twenty-five hundred years ago and still no one else has attained buddhahood. This is a difficult path to accomplish but not impossible, since we know that other sentient beings—bodhisattvas and liberated *arhats—have reached proximate buddhahood. So, by inference we can believe that buddhahood is attainable, but the only way is to generate the Four Great Vows and to practice the bodhisattva path. Indeed, one who practices the first three vows is already a bodhisattva, even though they have not yet attained buddhahood.

The first vow—to deliver sentient beings—is exemplified by the Buddha's last human life on this planet. He saw how sentient beings suffered through birth, sickness, old age, and death; he also saw how greed, hatred, and erroneous views created vexations. He therefore vowed to help us to overcome suffering. He left the princely life, became a mendicant, practiced, and, finally, reached buddhahood. His motivation was not to gain benefits for himself but to benefit sentient beings. This is the spirit of vowing to deliver all sentient beings, and this is compassion.

People may think, "Maybe the Buddha should have taken care of himself before benefiting sentient beings. If I were to take up this path, perhaps that would be more appropriate." This is an upside-down view because, if the Buddha did not generate the vow to help sentient beings, he would never have reached buddhahood; it is because he had this great compassionate vow and set out to practice that he reached buddhahood.

Bodhichitta and Renunciation

At the core of the Mahayana teachings are two related ideas: bodhichitta and renunciation. The Sanskrit "bodhichitta" can be translated as the "mind of [aspiration to] bodhi (enlightenment) for the sake of all sentient beings." Thus, giving rise to bodhichitta also means that one gives rise to great compassion. Renunciation is the aspiration to depart from affliction and the cycle of birth and death. Without bodhichitta and renunciation, it is difficult to practice the Mahayana path—they are like the two wheels of a bicycle: lacking either wheel, the bicycle cannot move, but with both wheels in proper alignment, the vehicle can move forward smoothly. Similarly, in one who has aroused compassion as well as the wish to end the cycle of birth and death, the two aspirations work together like the wheels of a bicycle.

The mind of great compassion, bodhichitta, also leads to the great vow to help sentient beings cross the sea of suffering. Yet, having such a vow requires one to also renounce attachment to sentient existence. So, one generates renunciation at the same time that they generate bodhichitta. Instead of flowing along in the endless stream of birth and death and getting caught in the whirlpool of suffering, one chooses the way of the Buddha with the wish that all sentient beings do the same. This is renunciation.

The *Parinirvana Sutra* and the *Avatamsaka Sutra* talk about the need to arouse bodhichitta as a means to attain buddhahood, but people cannot do this when they are burdened with vexations. The *Avatamsaka Sutra* also says that those who give rise to bodhichitta will eventually attain buddhahood. The *Sutra of Complete Enlightenment* says that sentient beings are already endowed with buddhahood. But if that is so, why aren't we all buddhas? It is because we are burdened with ignorance and vexation. How is it that the *Avatamsaka Sutra* says that once bodhichitta is aroused, we will eventually reach buddhahood? Because in giving rise to bodhichitta, we take the first step toward buddhahood. However, without generating this intention, no matter how hard we practice, enlightenment and buddhahood will be remote.

Since we have come here to practice, we already have a compassionate mind. But after arousing a mind to practice, people sometimes fall into wrong views or their practice becomes unstable and inconsistent. So, one day we give rise to bodhichitta and renunciation, and the next day we have forgotten all about them. Having wrong views can mean our mind has been turned by greed and seeking, and false renunciation can mean we are acting out of aversion to the world. We can aspire to buddhahood but become greedy in seeking that state, and with false renunciation we are perhaps doing it to escape from the world. Both attitudes are mistakes.

The Four Great Vows

These are the Four Great Vows that we recite daily: to deliver innumerable sentient beings, to sever all vexations, to master all Buddhadharma, to accomplish buddhahood. But this does not mean just chanting these vows; it means making them an integral part of our lives. For the first vow—delivering sentient beings—we have bodhichitta; for the second vow—cutting off vexations—we have renunciation. How do we deliver sentient beings, and how do we cut off vexations? That is accomplished with the third vow, mastering all approaches to Dharma. Through cultivating the Dharma, we can benefit others and cut off vexations. So, we see by this that bodhichitta and renunciation are inherent in fulfilling the vows. When we fulfill the first three vows, then we are fulfilling the fourth vow—attaining buddhahood. While practicing the Four Great Vows may be difficult, to fulfill them is to manifest bodhichitta in the most concrete way.

Sometimes we recite the vows without really meaning them. When we take these vows, we should say them from the depths of our heart so that we actually mean it. Some people fear making vows because they think the vows are too lofty for them to accomplish. They should know that the vows at least give us a direction and a path, and we try to fulfill them according to our own abilities and at our own pace.

People tell me to take it easier, to stop running around in the world lecturing and teaching, to retire. But I have not yet repaid my debts, and I have not yet fulfilled my vows. Therefore, I will continue beyond the limitations of this life, until I fulfill the vow of buddhahood. Beyond that, I rely on my body to take care of itself. My mind is at ease. Even though my body is aging, I can still drag it around and make use of it. So, if you can, give rise to bodhichitta to help others, and if you give rise to genuine renunciation, your vexations will also decrease.

I have a student who told me she does not think she can become a buddha. When I heard this, I assumed that was because she did not believe she possessed buddha-nature. But then she said, "Kshitigarbha Bodhisattva made a vow to deliver all the sentient beings in hell before becoming a buddha. In that case, who am I to think about becoming a buddha? There are so many sentient beings that need help; I want to help them before I can think about becoming a buddha." I realized then that in fact she had really given rise to bodhichitta. Free from self-preoccupation, she was more concerned with other people's welfare. When a person can truly generate bodhichitta, that person's character and life will be transformed; they will have less vexation and more compassion for others. So, when we generate bodhi-mind, even if we are not enlightened, we are in accordance with Buddhadharma.

Another student who had been studying with me for over ten years stopped coming to the center and attending retreats. When he showed up again, I asked him what happened. He replied, "Very honestly, I feel that I have learned everything you could teach me, so I didn't feel like coming anymore." I replied, "Yes, my Dharma is quite shallow, but coming here isn't just about learning something. Other people can use your help." When he heard this, he realized that he could be useful and started to come again. So, in either case, by giving rise to bodhichitta, these two people benefit others. Having bodhichitta, one can establish affinities with other beings and help them. If I cannot teach you the proper Dharma, that is to my shame, but it is still good for you to arouse bodhichitta and help others, as long as there is no arrogance.

So, from now on, when you sit, I wish all of you would make vows. You can make the Four Great Vows, repeating them to yourselves:

I vow to deliver all sentient beings.

I vow to cut off endless vexations.

I vow to master all approaches to the Dharma.

I vow to attain supreme buddhahood.

If you feel that these Four Great Vows are too lofty, then you can make the smaller vow of at least keeping your method before you at all times, and not lose it. Similarly, you can make vows in the midst of activities, such as, "May I walk and be free from vexations," or "When I see small creatures, may I give rise to compassion." In all activities, we can generate vows to guide such activities. Generating vows is bodhichitta, generating compassion is bodhichitta, being free from vexation is bodhichitta, and it is also renunciation and wisdom.

Attitudes for Practicing Chan

I would like to speak of three kinds of attitudes that are important for practicing Chan: compassion, renunciation, and detachment.

There is what I call "small compassion" and "great compassion," and both are different from empathy. Empathy is being sympathetic to someone else and is in relationship to oneself. For example, if you feel pity for someone, it is usually in reference to someone in a worse situation than you. This may cause you to reflect, "If I help out this person now, maybe one day when I am in need, somebody will then help me." This is empathy because it is self-referencing, and it is not Buddhist compassion.

Buddhist compassion is different from empathy in that it is felt from the standpoint of the Dharma. This means that in light of the Dharma, a person with compassion sees sentient beings as pitiable not because they are destitute, but because they are in the midst of afflictions they are not even aware of. One can only generate this kind of compassion when they understand the Dharma. So, from the perspective of the Buddhadharma, one is able to understand the workings of vexations within people and, from that realization, give rise to a genuine sense of pity.

In their afflicted state, sentient beings not only harm themselves but unknowingly harm others, directly or indirectly. The compassionate bodhisattva sees this very clearly and feels genuine pity. Specifically, they realize that sentient beings are in a state of unknowing and ignorance. "Unknowing" means people are unaware of how they are the cause of their own vexations and problems; "ignorance" means that in their afflicted state, they do not see the need to acquire wisdom to resolve their problems.

For this reason, bodhisattvas unconditionally devote themselves to helping sentient beings alleviate the causes for their pain and suffering. And yes, bodhisattvas should introspect to realize unknowing and ignorance within themselves. Upon seeing sentient beings' sufferings, bodhisattvas should reflect and realize that in their own mind are all sorts of vexations and wandering thoughts. Sometimes these thoughts are neither good nor bad, but other times it will be quite obvious that they are unwholesome. Being aware of one's own condition, they will try to reduce these causes of suffering within themselves to the lowest possible degree. In this manner, through seeing the suffering of others, bodhisattvas can reflect and see the causes of suffering in themselves.

Great compassion only manifests at the tenth ground, or *bhumi,* of the bodhisattva path, which is proximate buddhahood and beyond. So, only buddhas and great bodhisattvas like Avalokiteshvara embody great compassion. The bodhisattvas at this level do not have any thought of wanting to deliver sentient beings; in fact there is no subject who delivers sentient beings, nor sentient beings to be delivered. Yet, bodhisattvas spontaneously and naturally deliver sentient beings. This is great compassion.

Why is it that buddhas and great bodhisattvas can deliver sentient beings while holding no idea of delivering any sentient beings? It is because, being in a state of absolute selflessness, there can neither be any subject who delivers sentient beings, nor any objects called sentient beings to be delivered. Ordinary practitioners cannot generate this mind of great compassion, but we should still vow to cultivate selfless compassion and practice toward that.

Another prerequisite for practicing Chan is to cultivate renunciation. This does not mean we have to leave home and become monastics. Renunciation really means putting down attachments, being free and at ease. What kinds of attachments? Mainly, we put down attachments to gain, craving, hating, grasping, and rejecting. This requires diligent training because when one of these attitudes is present, inevitably the opposite mentality will also be present. When there is craving, there's hating; when there is seeking gain, there is fear of loss, and so on. Therefore we liberate ourselves from attachments by renouncing them and then training to put them down. Thus, we begin by renouncing attachments to ultimately become free of them.

If you have the attitude of detachment in your practice, whether you experience benefits or obstacles, you will be free and at ease. If you experience good things, you tell yourself they are impermanent and nothing to be proud of. If you have lots of wandering thoughts and obstacles and your practice is not smooth, that is also impermanent and there is no need to be upset. You can be free and at ease, and enlightenment is simply not an issue. So, you can practice with this attitude of understanding impermanence while having an attitude of detachment. And, at a moment of complete and utter detachment, it is possible to be liberated.

Emptying the Heart

When Zen Master Suzuki Roshi (1904–1971) was already old, he was asked why he was still actively teaching the Dharma. Suzuki replied that he just wanted to catch a few more fish. By this he meant he wanted to help a few more people onto the path. There are sixty-four of you here, and I believe none of you is a newcomer. But then if all of you have practiced with me before, why am *I* here? It cannot be said that I am trying to catch new fish since you are already practitioners. But you may say I am steaming half-cooked rice. What I mean is that while all of you have practiced before, most of you still look a little raw. So this rice needs to be cooked some more. When you reheat half-cooked rice, it gets mushy and doesn't taste that good. Nevertheless the effort must be made.

Whether you can become fully cooked of course depends partly on your karma. You came for various reasons: to lessen vexations, to learn a Chan method, even to reach enlightenment. But if you have not been using all you have learned in daily life, then the likelihood of your getting some benefit, not to mention becoming enlightened, is slim. If the best you can do is clear your mind a bit and rest your brains, you'll just go home and forget everything you learned here. That would be pitiable.

Before leaving, at least rekindle the fire of your practice, absorb the correct attitude, and apply it to daily life. Historically, daily life in Chan monasteries was distinct from other traditions—some encouraged solitary practice, some stressed silent contemplation, others emphasized ritual. What the ancient Chan masters emphasized was bringing the Dharma into daily life. That is the true spirit of Chan. So I encourage you to rekindle the fire and absorb the teachings on how to use huatou in each and every moment wherever you are.

Chan Master Dahui Zonggao guided eighteen people to enlightenment in a single night. This sounds very alluring, and you may think, "If I was there that night, perhaps I could have been enlightened!" You definitely shouldn't think like this. It was not the case that Dahui could do this every night! Impressive as this feat was, we can also wonder how many present did *not* get enlightened. That those eighteen had a glimpse of their buddha-nature is due solely to the causes and conditions for each of them.

According to the records of Dahui, over the years he was able to help many people see their buddha-nature. Enlightenment can be shallow, or it can be profound, but either way, the number of people that Dahui was able to guide to enlightenment would total nearly 2,800. The letters of Dahui also show that many of his correspondents were laypeople who gained insight, or as the Chan saying goes, "received some news from the enlightenment side."

Dahui had no secret technique, no esoteric teachings. He simply taught people how to investigate *wu*. That single word allowed him to freely bring people onto the path. The key is that in all situations, adverse or favorable, one should continuously bring forth *wu*. For example, in a troublesome situation your mind will not be at ease, but it is precisely then that you may gain an entry by picking up your huatou. On the other hand, if your practice is smooth, your mind clear and free from vexations, in that openness you may convince yourself that you are enlightened. In that event you should also bring forth *wu* lest you be enraptured by this idea. When you meet favorable situations, you must first tell yourself this is not "it" and quickly bring forth your huatou. All these situations, adverse or favorable, are delusions, definitely not awakening. So, in all situations that come up, just single-mindedly bring forth *wu*.

You could say that as a teacher Dahui used no expedient means other than *wu*. He also advised Chan people to empty their heart-mind. In Chinese, *xin* includes both the emotional aspect of the heart and the thinking aspect of the mind. So when we speak of heart here, we mean the larger sense of "heart-mind." This means you should embrace all of their concerns of body, mind, and environment with an empty heart, one that is spacious and without boundaries. With this kind of attitude, nothing can obstruct you. When using huatou, *wu* lives within your empty heart. In time it is possible that your mind will be in accord with buddha-nature.

Layman Pang (740–808), a famous Tang dynasty practitioner, said that one must empty their heart and not allow it to become solid. An empty heart does not attach to things, which would give them an illusion of solidity. When you attach to something, you believe it to be real, so the illusion of solidity becomes vivid and this creates an obstruction. You may give rise to jealousy, vexations, hatred, discontent, or desire, even wanting to reach enlightenment. So attaching to thoughts like these, how can your heart be empty? Without an empty heart, you are obstructed at every turn. If a mind is filled with narrow thoughts like these, even a grain of sand would be an obstruction. By comparison, the attitude of an empty heart is carefree and expansive.

You cannot generate an empty heart through practice; rather, it is an attitude that shapes your practice. This openness of heart is limitless because it is carefree and free-flowing. In that free flow you will not be caught up in anything, for everything, including *wu*, exists in this emptiness. A spacious room may contain objects, but you can still walk freely in it without being obstructed. With this kind of attitude, practice will go smoothly; nothing can impede your way; nothing can obscure *wu*. There will be times when you can't put down an obstruction because your mind is caught up with it. In this situation your heart cannot be said to be empty, and it will not be easy to empty it. So, when you hear talk about emptying one's heart, you may be tempted to say, "This is just the way it is, I can't put down my problem." In this case your heart has already solidified. The result is that you are blocked from making progress.

One of Dahui's students was a public official who wanted to know how he should practice in the midst of administrative matters. Dahui told him to deal with matters according to causes and conditions—that is to say, according to whatever required his attention and to flow with it. However, in the midst of activity, he must also earnestly bring forth *wu*. This way, the nuance of *wu* is likened to that of a spacious room in which *wu* can resonate with an emptiness that is free from care. So in essence, Dahui advised his student to act in accordance with causes and conditions while earnestly bringing forth *wu*.

Emptiness

There are misconceptions even among Buddhists about the meaning of emptiness as it pertains to enlightenment. After all, emptiness is the content, if you can call it that, of enlightenment. What is this emptiness? To what are we enlightened? Some people believe that they have experienced emptiness, while others have no idea what it is. In Buddhism there is the teaching of conditioned arising, which means that phenomena arise through the interplay of myriad causes and conditions. And, just as phenomena arise from causes and conditions, they perish through causes and conditions. Because causes and conditions are constantly changing, phenomena also constantly change. Being in constant flux, phenomena have no enduring self-entity and neither do sentient beings that also experience flux and change. On the human level, our impermanent existence leads to a pervasive sense of unease, which we call suffering. In Buddhism, the three so-called marks of existence—impermanence, suffering, and emptiness (no-self)—are intimately related. Things are impermanent because of causes and conditions, and because they are impermanent, this leads to suffering. Because things arise and perish due to conditioned arising, they have no inherent self-nature, and we call that emptiness.

We experience our own existence through time, but where is time? If space did not exist, there would be no way to experience or measure time. Because space and time are inseparable, together they define physical existence. If there were no body to experience time, even if time existed, it would be irrelevant. Time only becomes relevant when we experience our body existing in space. Thus, we can say that with this physical body comes time, and through this time we feel our own existence. Because we are conscious of our own existence in space-time, this gives rise to a sense of self, an "I" to which we attribute real existence. It is this "I" that gives rise to all sorts of problems.

From past to present to future, time is expressed in Buddhist teaching as a nexus of causes and effects: one thing leading to another in the temporal dimension. In other words, "cause and effect" is a description of existence. Causes and conditions exist in space, and we experience time as the current effects of prior causes. In turn, effects become causes to future effects, and the cycle continues. Spatially, cause can only lead to an effect if there are sufficient conditions to steer the outcome of events and things. So, cause and effect are conditioned by various causes and conditions in space. For this reason, this principal Buddhist teaching speaks of "conditioned arising" not "causal arising." If the causation was not influenced by conditions, then things would have constancy; they would not be impermanent. But because things are impermanent due to changing conditions, we call it "conditioned arising" instead of "causal arising."

To put it in simpler terms, we are aware of our own existence because we have a body. This body-sense is the coarsest level of the idea of self. Another aspect of the sense of self is that we experience the external environment as concrete and tangible; we exist relative to the world. Thus, external reality confirms our own existence.

Would we still have a sense of self if our body vanished and the environment vanished along with it? Yes, there could still be a very subtle form of self-grasping, unlike the coarseness of feeling our body and the environment. For example, in the deepest samadhi where one enters the formless realm and has gone beyond the fourth level (there are four levels to the formless realm of meditative absorption), there is neither sense of a body nor environment. Essentially, there's not even ordinary consciousness. In this extremely subtle state of consciousness where there is no body and no environment, how does the sense of self arise? To enter samadhi one uses an object of meditation; this object can be roughly spoken of as environment. So, in the beginning you meditate on something either external or internal. As we enter deep samadhi, the environment ceases to exist for us. So, what conditions are necessary for this subtle consciousness to give rise to a sense of self? The answer is that at that level the sense of self is self-perpetuating—it conditions itself in order to continue. At that moment, what is the self? It is neither the body nor the environment but the content of the

samadhi state itself. So, the self conditions the content of the samadhi to perpetuate itself. And what is the content of those states? At
the higher level of samadhi, the most subtle type of conscious state,
one experiences infinite spaciousness and nothing else. Although
we talk about time and space in samadhi as if they were infinite,
they exist for that practitioner. On the basis of this continuing experience of infinite spaciousness, the idea of a self experiencing this is
perpetuated. However, because there is attachment to existence, this
is still not liberation. Though the individual does not feel the existence of body or environment, there is still clinging to the infinite.
Spaciousness is really spaciousness, so this is grasping at existence.
In terms of samsara, this grasping will condition the mind to continued existence in the form of rebirth.

The state of a liberated arhat is beyond what I have just been
describing. Arhats who have entered nirvana experience neither
time nor space; indeed, if they were in time and space, they would
have a conditioned existence and be subject to rebirth. Therefore,
when they are liberated in nirvana, this is a total fusion with unconditioned emptiness, and for them there will be no rebirth. The goal
of the arhat path is to be liberated from samsara, so, upon achieving
nirvana, an arhat dwells in pure emptiness. It is extremely difficult,
though not impossible, for an arhat to choose to be reborn in order
to help sentient beings.

For Mahayana practitioners, so long as one can be free from
self-grasping, from attachment to self, at that very moment they
abide in emptiness and they can still be active in the world. In that
emptiness, which is inseparable from space and time, from inner
and outer, one can help sentient beings. The main point is to be
free from attachment of any kind, and that, for the bodhisattva, is
emptiness.

Chan teaches that at the very moment when one perceives
their self-nature—that is to say, the nature of emptiness—they are
liberated. When one experiences emptiness, at that time there is no

self, no "me" or "mine." When there are no vexations belonging to "you," that state is emptiness and liberation. In that state one also realizes the foolishness of giving rise to vexations, yet prior to that they were engulfed by them. So, enlightenment is the realization that this original quiescence has always been there; it is just that sentient beings contaminate this original mind with self-attachment. Until one experiences enlightenment, they will not know what this means. This is not to say that once enlightened, a person is forever liberated. Our habitual attachments are too strong to be eradicated by an initial enlightenment experience. After a short time, in most cases, a person who experiences enlightenment will give rise to attachment again and vexations will arise. For this reason, it is necessary to continue to practice. However, for a person who has the experience, she or he will recognize attachment and vexation when they arise, because she or he has already experienced the state free from self-attachment. This is very different from one who has never been freed from self-grasping.

What should you do right now? You should make use of the concepts and methods in accordance with the nature of emptiness. First, realize that your vexed condition is caused by yourself—you are the cause, and you are receiving your own effects. Nothing outside you is responsible for creating your problems for which you are now receiving the effects. Having this understanding, you should apply the concept of conditioned arising; you should apply the concept of impermanence. Whenever you experience negativity, consciously tell yourself, "This is impermanent and ultimately empty, and if I continue like this, I will cause my own suffering."

In terms of the practice, how do you gain a sense of emptiness? The point of entry is through understanding impermanence. You contemplate and you actually observe your mental processes. You see that just a moment ago a vexation wasn't there, and now you are suffering from it. Therefore, recognize that it is impermanent and without fundamental reality—in other words, empty. And a few moments later or in the future, it will also change. So, just by observing your changing states of mind, you gain a sense of that transience; you will directly experience this empty, fleeting nature of your own thoughts. That is how you accord with emptiness. So, both conceptually and in practice, you become intimate with the meaning of emptiness.

You can also do it in your daily life, learning to adapt to circumstances and regulating your afflictions. But you are only going to be successful later if you hone your skills now, while you are on retreat. You do not have to contemplate emptiness all the time, just when you become aware of vexations. Otherwise, I recommend you just stay with your huatou.

In Taiwan I had a monastic disciple who passed away from cancer. Toward the end of her life the painkillers simply did not work and the doctors could no longer help her. Only she could help herself, and so she recalled the retreat practice of contemplating emptiness. In the midst of excruciating pain, she contemplated emptiness and saw the insubstantial nature of her body and her pain; she saw them as conditions arising and perishing. Thus gaining a sense of emptiness, she was alleviated from pain and her mind was brought to a very calm state. She died a very peaceful, even joyful, death. Because this person practiced when she was healthy, when it came time to die, she knew how to deal with it.

PART TWO

COMMENTARIES ON HUATOU PRACTICE

THE ESSENTIALS OF PRACTICE AND ENLIGHTENMENT FOR BEGINNERS

*Commentary on a Text of
Chan Master Hanshan Deqing*

Concerning the causes and conditions of this great matter, this buddha-nature is intrinsically within everyone. As such, it is already complete within you, lacking nothing. The difficulty is that since time without beginning, seeds of passion, deluded thinking, emotional conceptualization, and deep-rooted habitual tendencies have obscured this marvelous luminosity. You cannot genuinely realize it, because you have been wallowing in remnant deluded thoughts of body, mind, and world, discriminating and musing about this and that. For these reasons, you have been roaming in the cycle of birth and death endlessly. Yet, all buddhas and ancestral masters have appeared in the world, using countless words and expedient means to expound on Chan and to clarify the doctrine, following and meeting different dispositions of sentient beings. All of these are expedient tools to crush our minds of clinging and enable them to realize that originally there is no substantiality to Dharma or sense of self.

What is commonly known as practice is simply to accord with whatever state of mind you're in, so as to purify and relinquish the deluded thoughts and traces of your habitual tendencies. Exerting your effort here is called practice. If within a single moment deluded thinking suddenly ceases, you will thoroughly perceive your own mind and realize it is vast and open, bright and luminous, intrinsically perfect and complete. This state, being originally pure, devoid of a single thing, is called enlightenment. Apart from this mind, there's no such thing as cultivation or enlightenment. The essence of your mind is like a mirror, and all the traces of deluded thoughts and clinging to conditions are defiling dust of the mind. Your conception of appearances or characteristics or forms is this dust, and your emotional consciousness is the defilement. If all the deluded thoughts melt again, the intrinsic essence will reveal itself of its own accord. It's like when defilements are polished away, the mirror regains its clarity. It is the same with Dharma.

However, our habits, defilements, and self-clinging are accumulated throughout aeons and have become solid and deep-rooted. Fortunately, having the guidance of a good spiritual friend is a causing condition that can influence our being, thus resulting in augmenting our internal prajna. Having realized that prajna [which is] inherent in us, we will be able to arouse the bodhi-mind and steer our direction toward the aspiration of relinquishing the cyclic existence of birth and death. This is the path of uprooting the roots of birth and death accumulated through aeons all at once in a subtle manner. If you are not someone with great strength and ability, brave enough to shoulder such a burden and to cut through directly to this matter without the slightest hesitation, then this task will be extremely difficult. An ancient one has said, "This matter is like one person confronting ten thousand enemies." These are not false words.

—from the DISCOURSE RECORD OF
MASTER HANSHAN DEQING

The Fragility of Life

The self that you are experiencing at this very moment is illusory and impermanent, and the sole purpose of huatou practice is to help you to discover the true self. To discover the true self, you must first be convinced that it indeed exists even though it is now covered by the illusory self. When we meditate we experience the illusory nature of the mind and through that, perhaps we gain some understanding that like our thoughts, the self is also illusory. Therefore, in terms of practice you must believe there is a true self waiting to be discovered. You can therefore use huatou as a tool to personally experience that true self.

To practice huatou well, you should be convinced of the fragility of life. You may have experienced the fragility of life if you have ever been at the threshold of death. You may also have witnessed the death of someone close to you, or even witnessed the death of strangers. These events make you realize how fragile your own life really is, and you come to understand that there must be something more than just this fleeting life. If that understanding leads you to practice, then you have taken a step toward finding meaningfulness in your life.

We can also observe the fleeting nature of life in the stream of illusory thoughts passing constantly through our mind. Does the real self exist in the gaps between these thoughts? The more you understand the transient nature of your thoughts, the more will be your urgency to find something not so transient: you say to yourself that there must be something more, and thus you come to the practice. With this kind of attitude you will practice well.

If you have already discovered that your deluded thoughts are not really you, then whatever method you have been using—breath-awareness, reciting the Buddha's name, or even a mantra—so long as you are able to calm the mind, you will gradually gain realization. When your mind becomes clearer and you reach a point where a quiet, subdued realization of impermanence arises, that is what we call "lightness-and-ease," or "mental pliancy." This mind is quite tranquil; it has experienced at some level its own insubstantial nature. This gradual approach is likened to a clay vessel containing muddy water in which the mud settles little by little until eventually the water is clear and transparent.

Using this kind of gradual approach is fine, but the huatou approach is not only a matter of gradually letting the mind settle down; rather, you use your full life force, like blowing at the water in the clay pot with great determination until there is no more water, nor any mud to settle. Better yet, using the power of huatou, you can shatter the clay vessel into a thousand pieces. All that will be left is an illuminated mind. Remember, this clay pot with muddy water is made by you, so you can use your strength to shatter it. You must have this urgency to discover something genuine and more fundamental than the illusory, transient self. With that in mind, there will be more power to your huatou.

You must be convinced that in your huatou you will discover your true life, your buddha-nature. Right now, you don't know what that is, but in the midst of this not knowing, you still believe that you are fully endowed with buddha-nature. Not knowing, you still want to know; you want to know what *wu* means. But if you conceive that "*wu* is buddha-nature," that is merely intellectual. Since *wu* means "nothing," how can you say it is a "thing"? You must investigate further, not being satisfied with any answer that you come up with; you must just continue to question, just continue to question.

At some point, being full of urgency, you might bang on the

floor. [*Demonstrates by banging on the floor*] This kind of urgency is like cornering a dog so it has no escape; you are convinced you can make it climb a wall. This is where you can give rise to the doubt sensation. At this point you should not give up, and you should also not say, "I know it! Yes! This is it!" You must reject this answer and press on.

To use our analogy, you must shatter the clay vessel so not a single drop of water is left. This can be likened to blowing away all your deluded thoughts to reach a state free from any thoughts. Please do not confuse this clear state with a merely blank mind that has been exhausted by fatigue. Having a mind that is aware and free of wandering thoughts is good; you are clear and have for now put aside all attachments. While it is not enlightenment, it is a good experience.

Student: When answers arise, you say we should reject them. Do we need to find a reason for denying them?

Sheng Yen: No, just put them aside. You don't have to rationalize why you reject the answers. As soon as you look for a reason for denying them, all the power you have accumulated will be lost and you will have trouble reconnecting with the continuous effort. So, as soon as these answers come up, just put them aside.

To repeat, to use the huatou method, you must have this existential concern about the fragility of life. This is the motivation that drives you on—realizing that life is transient and there must be a true self behind this illusory mind.

Points on Technique

As to technique, please do not synchronize asking the huatou with your breath. If you do that with urgency in your mind, you might end up breathing faster or inhaling and exhaling too deeply. All of this can cause breathing problems. So never practice your huatou as if it were a breathing method. Just focus on the question itself. Also, never use your thinking mind to find the answer to your huatou. Some people investigate the huatou by asking, "What is the answer? What is the answer?" And then they feel like their head is getting bigger and their chest is getting stuffy. This is a sign that they are using their brain too much. Do not conceptualize an answer; let the huatou itself give you the answer.

Do not just recite the huatou as if it were a mantra; give it a flavor of urgent questioning: [*Demonstrating*] "What is *wu*? What is *wu*?" The tempo or pace is up to you; you can adjust it to your own rhythm. The main point is not to allow thoughts to arise in the gap between one asking and the next. Between the gaps, just maintain the flavor of questioning with a wondering attitude and just keep doing that. Your practice must be smooth, without allowing thoughts to seep into the space between asking. Just continue to ask the huatou, and keep asking. Now, the gaps between asking can very well extend to even a minute or more, so long as no wandering thoughts or distractions seep in. You can ask, "What is *wu*?" and then maintaining the flavor for a while, again ask later, "What is *wu*?"

Beginners may find it difficult to free themselves from distracting thoughts, but it may be because they are asking the huatou at too rapid a pace: [*Imitating reciting quickly*] "What is *wu*? What is it? What is *wu*? What is *wu*?" If you find yourself becoming tense like this, you can temporarily put aside the method, relax, make your mind joyful, and then resume asking. If you find yourself becoming exhausted, that is a sign that you've asked the question in a tense way, and you should avoid that. The point is continuing to ask with consistency and being free from distracting thoughts.

Maintain the intention of wanting to know; indeed, without this wanting to know, you may as well recite a mantra. The point is that you want to know the answer to the huatou. If you find yourself becoming tired, then just relax and temporarily put aside the method. If while resting, you keep your mind free from distraction, that is good enough until you recuperate a bit and you can resume.

By all means, if you arrive at a crucial point at which the doubt can appear, just focus on that. At that point you don't have to repeat anything. Just maintaining the flavor itself is sufficient if you can do it. But I would suggest that once in a while you repeat the whole phrase, so you don't become lost in a samadhi-like state. This will also help to refresh the doubt sensation. The whole idea is to maintain a continuously questioning mind.

Using the Vajra Sword to Kill Delusions

In Chan, we say that practicing huatou is like having a *vajra* sword, a diamond sword, that cuts through delusion and attachment. When attachment to self stands in the way of realization, we use the vajra sword to slice through that attachment. When Buddhadharma confronts the sword, the sword can also slice through it. In the scriptures there is a story that as the Buddha was giving a sermon, the bodhisattva Manjushri appeared with a vajra sword and chased the Buddha away. This is possible because the vajra sword is extremely sharp and extremely hard and cuts through even clinging to the Buddhadharma. Indeed, the vajra sword is the sword of wisdom that can sweep away anything that comes before it.

While practicing huatou is like having a vajra sword, you must still have faith and confidence in the method. Since you came to a huatou retreat, you must already have some belief in this method. And if you have faith in this method, you don't have to justify it with reasons, because it is just this habit of reasoning that the vajra sword cuts away. For example, in some approaches to practice, when you recognize a vexation, you can say, "Such and such is a vexation; therefore, I will let it go." Then, another vexation arises: "Yes, I will not be involved with that, because that is a vexation." Vexations arise because they are deeply embedded in the mind. They can be quite lovely and quite pleasurable, and because they exist as subtle clinging, they arise again and again. So, in the huatou method we use the king of all diamond swords to cut off whatever arises, whether pleasurable or not, lovely or not; we just cut it off with the vajra sword. This is the direct approach.

In a famous Chan story, Master Xiangyan (d. 898) tells about a monk hanging by the teeth to a tree branch that hangs over a steep cliff. While the monk is hanging there, someone asks the monk, "What is the meaning of Bodhidharma coming from the West?" If the monk doesn't answer, he has failed to help a sentient being; if he answers, he falls to his death. What should the monk do?

We are somewhat like that monk who is afraid to speak: if we don't commit to the practice, then we should not be Chan practitioners. In interviews, some of you have expressed some fear about practicing huatou: "If I continue working on the huatou like this, I'm afraid of what will happen to me." Well, you should not be afraid. At least there's no tree branch hanging over a cliff; as you can see, we are on level ground. So even if you decide to let go, there is no cliff to fall from.

Some of the questions tell me you are not entirely clear about the huatou method or sufficiently confident about its purpose. The purpose of the huatou method is to help you sever your attachments, your clinging, and your vexations, and most importantly, your illusory mind. Now you may say, "All I want is a little bliss; I just want to meditate and be happy. I didn't come here to give up my life to this huatou method." If you have this attitude, that is understandable. But to that I will reply—precisely because you want to be happy and you want to be serene when confronting death—that you should practice huatou.

Giving Rise to the Doubt Sensation

After you have gained some confidence and faith in the practice, you must work hard to give rise to the great doubt. This doubt is not suspicion as opposed to belief. It is what Chan calls the "doubt sensation." Having great faith means you believe you are fully endowed with buddha-nature and that you are able to become enlightened. After all, these beliefs were spoken of by the Buddha himself and testified to by the lineage masters. And here I am encouraging you and stating this as true. I have offered you some water to quench your thirst, but it is up to you to drink it. If you wonder if water can really quench your thirst, this is suspicion, not Chan doubt. So, if you believe, "Yes, water can quench my thirst, and I will drink it," this is faith. After you act on this faith and engage in continuously asking the huatou, you will give rise to a strong sense of wanting to know the answer. You will know very well that the huatou *can* give you an answer though, as of now, you don't know what that is. So, if you believe that there is an answer to the huatou, this sense of questioning is the doubt sensation.

Someone once asked me, "Is there buddha-nature? Is enlightenment attainable?" I replied, "It is because people do not believe in buddha-nature that they cannot become enlightened." I encouraged her to develop confidence and faith, because a person who has them will at least have a chance at enlightenment; without faith there is little chance. So, if you believe in buddha-nature, the chances of becoming enlightened are much better than if you do not believe. So first, establish your faith.

With regard to the doubt sensation, there are three stages. At the first stage, on the basis of faith and confidence, you earnestly ask, "What is *wu*?" You want to know the answer very badly, but at this stage, instead of allowing the huatou to reveal the answer, you use your thinking mind. Any answers you come up with will be wrong precisely because they are based on thinking. But at this first stage at least you have a sincere desire to know the answer.

In the second stage of the doubt sensation you feel a strong attraction to the huatou, as if it were pulling at you like a magnet, compelling you to ask the question. Again and again, you continually ask the question not because you intentionally want to ask but because there is a strong attraction, a strong flavor to it. Similarly, the relationship between you and the huatou is like this; you are greatly interested in it and being pulled by it. So you ask the huatou again and again, continuously, without gaps. In the first stage you may lose the huatou now and then before picking it up again. But in the second stage the wanting-to-know is continuous, and the only way you can lose the huatou is if you become too tired to sustain the focus.

In the third stage of the doubt sensation you are fully engulfed in the doubt—the sense of deeply wanting to know—to the extent you are no longer reciting the huatou. Rather, you are completely absorbed in this "great ball of doubt." You are not asking as if it were something outside you; rather, you *are* this great mass of doubt, and you want to know the answer very badly. This state can last as briefly as a few minutes or as long as a day, a few days, weeks, months. In this state you can still perform ordinary functions like eating, walking, and sleeping, but these are done inside this great ball of questioning and there is no other thought except the word-less asking of the huatou. Do not be afraid of this state, because, in the first place, most people cannot reach it. But if you do, you can stay on here and we will take care of you. While you are within this great doubt mass, complicated tasks like driving a car are out of the question. If you had an accident, the first thing you might ask the other person is, "What is *wu*?" [*Laughter*] That poor person will be completely dumbfounded.

A high school math teacher in Taiwan who attended a huatou retreat practiced quite well from beginning to end. When he went home, he rested for just one day and then went back to school. He was writing some equations on the board when all of a sudden he turned around and asked in a loud voice, "Who am I?" [*Laughter*] But this third stage is difficult to reach, so don't worry about it. Just work on your practice!

To work well on the huatou method, you must give rise to the doubt sensation, because that is the whole point. Of course, if you just recite the huatou without raising the doubt mass, that will still be useful for settling your mind. At most you may be able to enter a one-pointed samadhi, but by itself samadhi will not lead to enlightenment, whereas raising and resolving the doubt mass can. In the Linji tradition of Chan, there is this saying: "Big doubt, big enlightenment; small doubt, small enlightenment; no doubt, no enlightenment."

Some people practice huatou with a lot of tension and become fatigued as a result. In fact when it comes to practice, by using your energy wisely, you gain energy. Huatou is really an easy practice. For example, when having a conversation, you have to think about what you're going to say. With huatou practice you have nothing to think about except to ask the question. There is no other burden or consideration on your part. You keep asking the huatou, and it will give you the answer. So you should practice huatou in a relaxed manner.

Some students practice huatou as if it were some kind of an enemy they are trying to defeat. Why should you treat something that is going to make you a buddha like that? No, you should treat the huatou as your best friend, a most trustworthy, most reliable friend who is going to bring you to buddhahood. So, very kindly and very sincerely think of your huatou as a dear friend, and take good care of that relationship.

One time a student was investigating his huatou very intensely and very painfully. When he saw me, he grabbed me, shook me, and shouted, "Shifu! Tell me the answer!" He was acting as if I were some kind of adversary. I asked him, "Are you investigating the huatou, or are you investigating me?" [*Laughter*]

He said in desperation, "You gave me this huatou and brought me so much pain and misery. I just don't know the answer!"

I told him that practicing huatou is like planting a single seed that eventually sprouts, grows into a tree bearing leaves, flowers, and eventually bears fruit. Finally, you harvest the fruit and eat it. So there are a lot of causes and conditions at work, a lot of factors at play here. I am merely someone who gives you the seed that has the full potential to grow into a tree bearing fruit.

I said, "I give you this seed, and already you are demanding a taste of the fruit. This is not reasonable."

He said, "Shifu, didn't you say that investigating Chan is a matter of sudden enlightenment? What is all this stuff about causes and conditions?"

Do you all have questions like that? There are three attitudes that should be present here: one must be patient, one must be diligent, and one must have confidence. Having confidence, you work on it with diligence, while maintaining patience. I hope that none of you will grab me by the shoulders, demanding an answer to their huatou. [Laughter]

In Chinese, huatou is a compound word meaning the "head of a saying." Of course, the words in a huatou are just words; they cannot provide you with any answer. But yet, in your questioning, you must find an answer, and you have faith that there is an answer. If you give rise to great doubt, the source behind these words will eventually reveal an answer, and discovery will be wisdom.

Here is a story that may illustrate this: There was a wise elder named Chang who used to go fishing with a pole, but at the end of the line he did not have bait or even a hook. Yet, he was out there fishing all day long. One day, the emperor, who had heard about Chang, sent a messenger to seek out this wise person. As soon as Chang saw the messenger, he said, "Oh, the big fish does not come; instead he sends a little fish!" The messenger went back to the emperor with this message, and sure enough one day the emperor himself showed up. Chang said to the emperor, "Aha! Finally, the big fish has come." So, similarly, fishing without a hook is like the huatou method—just an expedient means to catch a very big fish. So, I see lots of fish in here, lots of big fish waiting to be caught. [Laughter]

Beginner's Mind

I want now to take up a text by Chan Master Hanshan Deqing (1546–1623) on "The Essentials of Practice and Enlightenment for Beginners" from *The Discourse Record*. The specific topic that Hanshan addresses in this text is the beginner's mind. In Chinese, this is *chuxin,* which has two meanings. The first meaning is fairly obvious and refers to the mind of someone who just embarked on the practice. The second is something more profound: it says that however long you have been practicing, you should always keep a mind that is fresh from moment to moment, facing whatever confronts you, whether you have practiced for ten, twenty, fifty, a hundred years. None of you have practiced for a hundred years, but even if you had, you should view practice as if you were just starting out fresh. Thus, the scriptures place great emphasis on the bodhisattva's initial generation of bodhichitta being constantly renewed with vows.

The saddest thing in practice is to have gained very little and to be self-satisfied and content with that. So, these two Chinese words, "beginner's mind," also have a nuance of humility. For example, if someone has been practicing for a very long time yet still is humble, still thinking he or she is just beginning anew, then that person can truly be called a bodhisattva.

I once brought a well-educated Taiwanese politician to see one of my lineage masters, Lingyuan (1902–1988). At one point this politician asked the master, "How old are you?"

And Master Lingyuan answered, "I should be ashamed. I am already seventy years young."

The visitor asked the master, "How long have you been practicing?"

Master Lingyuan answered, "I don't consider the things I do practice. We can't really talk about practice with regard to what I do."

So, the congressman continued to seek some teaching. He said,

"Master, I have traveled from afar to come here. I wish to receive some teaching so, when I leave, I can take your Dharma and put it to use."

Master Lingyuan replied, "Dharma? Look at me. Do I look like someone who knows Buddhadharma? Then again, you've received higher education from abroad. I should ask you to teach me some Dharma."

Master Lingyuan then said, "I'm tired now. Good-bye!" And then he just went to his room to rest.

The congressman then said to me, "I have learned much today."

I was curious and asked, "What did you learn?"

He said, "I came to hear your master expound the Dharma, but he was so humble; he did not try to impress me with his Dharma. That's indeed something to emulate. I have witnessed the Chan saying of going 'beyond words and language.' Today I have really met a very accomplished master."

Later, I asked Master Lingyuan, "When I brought this congressman to see you, why didn't you speak any Dharma to him?"

He said, "What did you want me to say? You know these educated people—whatever I say, they will refute it, so I shut up." [*Laughter*]

So, unlike Master Lingyuan, when students ask me questions, I try to answer them directly, and that is why I get arguments from some of my students. [*Laughter*]

So, let's proceed to the text: "The Essentials of Practice and Enlightenment for Beginners."

Concerning the causes and conditions of this great matter, this buddha-nature is intrinsically within everyone. As such, it is already complete within you, lacking nothing. The difficulty is that since time without beginning, seeds of passion, deluded thinking, emotional conceptualization, and deep-rooted habitual tendencies have obscured this marvelous luminosity. You cannot genuinely realize it, because you have been wallowing in remnant deluded thoughts of body, mind, and world, discriminating and musing about this and that. For these reasons, you have been roaming in the cycle of birth and death endlessly. Yet, all buddhas and ancestral masters have appeared in the world, using countless words and expedient means to expound on Chan and to clarify the doctrine, following and meeting different dispositions of sentient beings. All of these are expedient tools to crush our minds of clinging and enable them to realize that originally there is no substantiality to Dharma or sense of self.

This text by Hanshan says that we are fully endowed with faith in our original nature as a buddha, but that faith is obscured by ignorance and the passions. Hanshan assures us that the buddhas have appeared in the world to give us the "expedient means" to help to us "crush our minds of clinging" to realize original nature. Whether or not someone engages in Buddhist practice, everyone has this original faith. Yet, while this is so, the habitual accumulation of passions over many lifetimes has completely obscured this original faith in our buddhahood, so that even a serious practitioner has difficulty realizing this original faith. The difficulty is because, since time without beginning, we have been indulging in the traces from the past of the body, mind, and world, giving rise to all sorts of false notions and clinging. Therefore, we have been cycling through endless rounds of birth and death.

Since Shakyamuni Buddha, generations of lineage masters have appeared in the world, speaking the Dharma according to people's dispositions, so that sentient beings can sever their grasping to these remnant traces. We should understand that there is no fixed Dharma to give; rather, depending on people's karmic potential and level of practice, the ancestors taught different approaches to Dharma. So, essentially there is no fixed Dharma—all the different words of the Dharma are just expedient means.

Now I will tell a story about my other lineage master, Dongchu (1908–1977). In 1976 he came to the United States to visit me. At that time, a layman invited us to his place and treated us with great hospitality. During the day he said to Master Dongchu, "Tonight, I hope I will be able to hear some Dharma teachings." And there I was in the middle, thinking, "Well, tonight is going to be a big event. On the one hand there's my teacher Dongchu, and on the other hand, a famous layperson knowledgeable in Buddhism. I can't wait to hear what they are going to talk about."

And then the time arrived, all three of us sitting there. And our host said to Master Dongchu, "Master, please expound some teaching." And Master Dongchu said, "Well, first, thank you very much for being our host, and thank you very much for helping my disciple come to America, and also, thank you very much for helping spread Dharma in the West, so that many people will benefit."

Very politely our host said, "Oh, don't thank me for any of that. That is just what I should be doing."

And then the two started chatting about some trivial things. There I was, witnessing these two involved in chitchat, and after about an hour, Master Dongchu started yawning, and our host said, "Master, you must still have jet lag; you should rest."

And Dongchu said, "Thank you, thank you. Yes, indeed, I should take a rest." And that was it.

So, I accompanied Master Dongchu to his bedroom. I said to him, "You didn't give our host any Dharma; you just talked about meaningless stuff."

Master Dongchu turned around and looked at me. "You are just a youngster, what do *you* know?!" [*Laughter*] He continued, "The more you discuss Dharma, the more misunderstanding you create, so you might as well talk about meaningless things."

The Chan elders are often like this, so next time when you want to hear some Dharma, like tomorrow morning, I'll just do chitchat. [*Laughter*] Chan is indeed like this—it is not separate from mundane life. Chitchat is not that far different from talking about some great principle of Dharma. When you discuss Dharma, anything said could end up being off the mark. So, when you meet very knowledgeable, intelligent people, my advice is not to discuss Buddhadharma. If you have some special debating skill in Chan you can easily show off and impress people, but if you don't have anything to demonstrate directly without words or language, then it is best to just hide your knowledge.

At the old Chan Center in Queens, New York, some Chinese people visited me. Right off, one of them said, "Master Sheng Yen, have you read this very famous book, *The Five Lamps Merging at the Source?*"

This is a very famous text, the five lamps referring to the five lines of Chan. So, I said: "Sounds familiar, but I can't say I know it well."

Very bluntly, this person said, "Are you teaching Chan here? Are you enlightened?"

I said, "I don't know if I'm enlightened."

Then he said, "Well, in this book there is this one line, 'It goes from dawn to dusk.' What is the meaning of this line?"

And there I was scratching my head, repeating, "'It goes from dawn to dusk . . . from dawn to dusk.' Sorry, I don't know what that means."

"You're not enlightened, then?"

And I replied, "Thank you for reminding me."

And they left very disappointed. Originally they came, probably prepared with a whole bunch of questions. And when they realized that I was not enlightened, I actually saved myself from having to debate a lot of questions! [*Laughter*]

Now we'll return to the text where it says bodhisattvas and

lineage masters appear in the world, using countless ways to expound the doctrine, using all sorts of expedient means. What the lineage masters say is not actually Dharma, since the Dharma itself is not expressible in words; they are only expediencies to help people. So, when we confront these different teachings, it is pointless to debate which one is genuine, which one is correct. It is correct and genuine when it is useful for that particular individual.

The text continues:

> What is commonly known as practice is simply to accord with whatever state of mind you're in, so as to purify and relinquish the deluded thoughts and traces of your habit tendencies. Exerting your effort here is called practice. If within a single moment deluded thinking suddenly ceases, you will thoroughly perceive your own mind and realize it is vast and open, bright and luminous, intrinsically perfect and complete. This state, being originally pure, devoid of a single thing, is called enlightenment. Apart from this mind, there's no such thing as cultivation or enlightenment. The essence of your mind is like a mirror, and all the traces of deluded thoughts and clinging to conditions are defiling dust of the mind. Your conception of appearances or characteristics or forms is this dust, and your emotional consciousness is the defilement. If all the deluded thoughts melt again, the intrinsic essence will reveal itself of its own accord. It's like when defilements are polished away, the mirror regains its clarity. It is the same with Dharma.

This paragraph makes three main points. The first is that to practice means relinquishing our deluded thinking as well as the habits that keep us in the cycle of birth and death. If we can free ourselves of these patterns or propensities that propel us to act in certain ways, then there is no other thing called practice. The second point is that there is no such thing as enlightenment; it is not as if you suddenly realize some great, marvelous thing or truth. Enlightenment is just a state devoid of deluded thinking and attachments. But once these things are relinquished, that is already enlightenment. It's not some thing or object that you realize. For the third point, Hanshan uses the analogy of a mirror: practice— meaning relinquishing bad habits, karmic propensities, and deluded thinking—is like keeping a mirror clean of the accumulated defilements of the mind, what Chan calls "dust." Essentially, practice entails this continuous process of polishing the mirror-mind.

Relating this to huatou practice, many people misuse the method. The first type sees the huatou as an adversary to be overcome, so success means they win and their huatou loses. This is a misuse of huatou because, with this attitude, they are constantly opposing the huatou. It is impossible to reach enlightenment with this kind of attitude.

There's another type of practitioner who misuses the huatou by being too greedy. They recite and ask the huatou, treating it as a friend. But then they seek out some kind of bargain with this huatou, holding back on giving their best effort in return for just a little bit of realization, perhaps just a taste of enlightenment. "Just let me have a little bit, I just want to know what it tastes like." Since *wu* means "nothing," how can asking, "What is nothing?" bring about enlightenment? In fact, it is very difficult for a person who seeks enlightenment to attain it, no matter what method they are using. The true way to use huatou is as a tool to free the mind of the traces of deluded thinking. The more you give them up the better, until self-clinging and self-attachment vanish.

A third misuse of the method is to become afraid of it. Some people wonder, "What will happen if I keep asking the huatou?" They don't know what's going to happen if they continue the questioning, and they are afraid of that. There's a story of a woman who was extremely beautiful but didn't know it because she was born blind. Her husband, on the other hand, is extremely ugly. He has taken care of her tenderly and with lots of love. One day he found a doctor who could cure her blindness. At first he thought, "If she is cured, she will see that I am ugly and will not love me any more." But the second voice in his head said, "You love her, and it's your duty to help her to see." So he said, "OK, that's it. I love her and want her to see, so I don't care what her response will be."

So, this is like a huatou practice. Right now, like this ugly man, some of you are afraid of what will happen when you dedicate yourself to the practice of huatou. However, when you discover your buddha-nature, you will see just exactly who you are, with one exception: The good news is that unlike the analogy, your ugliness has vanished. So, for this reason, do not be afraid of seeing your original face for the first time.

Practicing Mu at Twenty-Seven below Zero

Perhaps it's just my advanced age, but tonight I feel very cold in here. I remember when I was younger and attending *sesshin* (Zen retreat) in Japan, and it was twenty-seven below zero, but I was able to bear it. And now, [in Pine Bush, New York, late in December], it is only ten below outside, and I already feel cold. Here we have baseboard heating and insulated windows, but over there it was just two sheets of *shoji* (paper screen) serving as a wall; the inner shoji was very thin, the outer one was a little bit thicker and waterproof. There was no heat and the snow outside covered the window. Well, that is a bit of an exaggeration. From inside it looked like the snow was up to the top of the window, but probably the snow only came to the bottom of the window. Snowdrifts had covered the window-panes; therefore when you looked out, it felt like it was all snow.

The *zendo* was designed such that between the two shoji layers there was a walkway. The outer layer of thicker waterproof shoji was about four or five feet from the thin inner layer that we sat against, and that design warded off some of the coldness. But it was still very cold. In the zendo the monks were all practicing *wato* (Japanese for "huatou") and reciting out loud, "*Mu!*" (Japanese for *wu*). At times I felt like I was sitting among a herd of cows, with *mu*'s coming from here and *mu*'s coming from over there. [*Laughter*]

When I first arrived, hearing this, I thought, "These monks are really making an all-out effort to get enlightened." After the sesshin, I remarked to one of them, "You folks were practicing *mu* constantly and so hard, you must all be enlightened." He said, "Not at all, we were just cold." [*Laughter*]

We slept on *tatami* (straw mats), and of course there was no heat. There was no pad to cover the cold tatami, but they did give us a blanket. The interesting part about this blanket was that when you covered your chest, your feet were exposed, and when you covered your feet, your chest was exposed. [*Laughter*] This must have been a specially designed blanket because it was impossible to be comfortable with it, so you had to remain awake and practice *mu* all night. [*Laughter*] That's why, as soon as the boards clapped in the morning, everyone got up immediately. No one wanted to stay under the blanket.

Anyone here experience this kind of sesshin before?

Student: No, but I think I will sleep outside tonight. [*Laughter*]

Sheng Yen: Practicing in the middle of such cold has its uses. First of all, you can develop lots of willpower, and secondly, you cannot fall asleep. It would be impossible to doze off, but most people probably would not last one day. A lot of us here are wearing woolen caps, but the Japanese were bald and bareheaded, no caps. After they washed their faces very quickly in icy water, they would pant like this [*twice makes three loud panting sounds*]. [*In English*] No need for translation. [*In Chinese*] When they wiped themselves with a wet towel, you could see steam coming off their faces. What was interesting was that no one caught cold. It was too cold to catch a cold.

Attending a retreat like this is inconceivable to most people.

Even though you may not get enlightened, afterward you feel like you have been through a real retreat. [*Laughter*] For you young people, it would be a good thing to experience one of these retreats.

Doing Battle with the Ten Thousand Enemies

Now that the fun is over, let's continue with Hanshan's admonitions on how to practice to enlightenment. The text continues:

> However, our habits, defilements, and self-clinging are accumulated throughout aeons and have become solid and deep-rooted. Fortunately, having the guidance of a good spiritual friend is a causing condition that can influence our being, thus resulting in augmenting our internal prajna. Having realized that prajna [which is] inherent in us, we will be able to arouse the bodhi-mind and steer our direction toward the aspiration of relinquishing the cyclic existence of birth and death. This is the path of uprooting the roots of birth and death accumulated through aeons all at once in a subtle manner. If you are not someone with great strength and ability, brave enough to shoulder such a burden and to cut through directly to this matter without the slightest hesitation, then this task will be extremely difficult. An ancient one has said, "This matter is like one person confronting ten thousand enemies." These are not false words.

In this excerpt, Hanshan is saying two things. First, through many kalpas (countless aeons) we have accumulated so many deep-rooted delusions and bad habits that they have completely obscured our intrinsic wisdom. And because these delusions and attachments have been there for so long, it is very difficult to uproot them all at once. But just as good fortune brings you to retreat, likewise, your inherent wisdom has been stirred by good karmic roots, steering you to practice Buddhadharma. Not only is your inherent prajna set in motion by good karma, but you have been able to meet "good spiritual friends"—teachers who point out the way toward enlightenment.

Hanshan next tells us that the path to buddhahood is quite a difficult one to travel; he says that if you do not have full conviction as well as great determination, you will not persevere. He gives an analogy of someone dashing forward alone to confront ten thousand enemy soldiers. If a practitioner does not have this mind of great determination and great willpower to embark on the practice, then they will not be able to complete the path. So, a true practitioner is someone brave, determined, and strong enough to sever their vexations and afflictions, like one warrior facing ten thousand enemies.

A closer translation of this line about the enemies would have been: "This matter is like one bare-chested person facing ten thousand enemies." "Bare-chested" here means that this brave individual goes forward to battle without wearing protective armor. So, this is the kind of attitude that a Chan adept should have—great determination, great will, and great strength.

This reminds me of my experiences of sesshin in Japan. In the Chinese Chan tradition, practice has more to do with a mental attitude, a spirit for practice rather than overcoming adverse external conditions. It seems to me that the Japanese Zen tradition has taken up this spirit and externalized it, so that coping with very harsh conditions like winter is like "one person facing ten thousand enemies." Is this useful? Practitioners would probably not get enlightened under such circumstances, but nevertheless they would develop a tremendous amount of will, determination, and forbearance; they have undergone so much hardship that it is like being a samurai. Every one of those practitioners emerges from sesshin as if from Mount Fuji, stern and ready to do battle.

When I returned to Taiwan from Japan, people told me, "You look Japanese." In fact, I felt Japanese; after all, I had spent a little bit over six years in Japan, staying with the people and doing sesshin with them. Thus, when I returned to Taiwan, people felt that I had an air about me that was Japanese. But people do not say that anymore.

Now, when some people meet me, they may say, "Are you really a Chan master? You look too frail to be a Chan master." They have an idea that Chan masters should be so powerful and so stern. One person who was really quite remote from looking like a Chan master was my Linji lineage master, Lingyuan. On first meeting, you would not guess this unassuming fellow was a Chan master at all. Compared to him, at least I sometimes try to look like a Chan master. [*Laughter*]

This section of the text is very important, for it tells us we should straightaway take up the burden of practice, and whatever we confront, we should face it fully. If we make a mistake, there is no regret. We also take up this responsibility fully. When you take up this method, apply it directly and move forward without regret. Otherwise, the slightest doubt, the slightest suspicion, and the ten thousand enemies will defeat you: "Is this method suitable for me? I've been using it for half a day now and nothing is happening. Maybe I should try something else." Instead of dashing forward sword in hand to confront the enemy, you start thinking about this or that reason why you should not. With these second thoughts, you will be vanquished right then and there.

So, when it comes to practice, do not doubt whether the method is right for you. Pick up your weapon of prajna and advance. Moreover, when you engage in the practice, remember that these ten thousand enemies are not outside your own mind; they are your own deluded thoughts, your discriminations, your self-deprecations, your wandering thoughts, your clinging, your jealousies, you name it. Whatever you can identify as afflictions, those emotions and thoughts are the ten thousand enemies at the gate. But "ten thousand" is just a figure of speech: in fact our negative emotions, afflictions, and vexations are without number.

Fortunately, the sword that you have in your hand, your huatou, is no ordinary sword; it is the vajra sword of wisdom, the sword of Vajradeva, the Diamond King, which is able to cut through delusions with one swift stroke. The safest way to confront the ten thousand enemies in your mind is to pick up that sword and without blinking an eye, slash your way through—just cut them down. And then you will be safe. Otherwise, if you hesitate—"Should I really kill this delusion?"—you will be defeated. And what are these delusions? They are any thoughts that are not your huatou.

An analogy that is sometimes used to describe huatou practice goes something like this: "The myriad thoughts are snowflakes drifting down from the sky; they fall into a volcano that is boiling with molten lava." So what are the chances of these snowflakes surviving? Put in terms of practice, however many wandering and deluded thoughts we have, they will be evaporated by the roaring flame of the huatou. The boiling lava, gathering up tremendous energy, is not afraid of wandering thoughts or deluded thinking. Whatever lands on it is melted away.

In the old days, a retreat in China was much more difficult than it is here. Over here, we get up at four in the morning and sleep at ten o'clock. That is six hours of rest. Back then, it was a longer day, and it was much more difficult to sustain the practice. You would sleep probably four hours. By nine at night people were already exhausted after a hard day of meditation and work. Back then it was not the abbot or the master who scolded the practitioners— it was usually a senior monk who sat in the first seat of the Chan Hall—someone like Guoyuan *Fashi, who is sitting here. Typically, he would shout things like, "The demon *Mara is confronting you! You are about to die!" and such expressions. This kind of exhortation might go on for an hour. During this scolding and shouting at the practitioners, the whole Chan Hall would echo with the words. Anyone who was dozing off would wake up immediately. The effect was better than tapping on people's shoulders with the *incense board to wake them up.

[*Shouts*] "Death waits for no one! It can happen at any time! Sleeping in the Chan Hall again?"

[*In a normal voice*] The typical practitioner hearing this would give rise to great energy and continue with the practice. An interesting note is that they usually saved the first seat for someone with a very loud voice, a very good, clear voice. Guoyuan Fashi here has a very good voice. You just haven't heard him really shout yet.

Guoyuan Fashi: [*In English*] In the West it's more difficult because I would have to yell in two languages, but it would lose something in translation. [*Laughter*]

Sheng Yen: [*In English*] Don't worry, just use English. [*Laughter*] In fact, the practitioners did not have to understand what the first seat was saying. He just had to roar.

Guogu (the translator): [*In English*] Tomorrow it is my turn to yell at you folks.

Sheng Yen: Don't scare them too much or they will not come back for another retreat. [*Laughter*]

What do you think the essence of tonight's teaching was? What should we bring forth in our practice?

Student: Endurance.

Sheng Yen: Endurance. Anything else?

Student: How would you compare huatou with Silent Illumination practice?

Sheng Yen: The spirit of practicing huatou is very different from that of Silent Illumination. Silent Illumination is a very difficult method. With huatou, you just pick up the vajra sword of wisdom and cut away at deluded thoughts. Whatever you see, kill it; it's as easy as that. There is no skill to practicing huatou. [*Laughter*]

OK, that's it for tonight. Tomorrow is the last day, practice hard.

AN EXCERPT FROM *IMPETUS TO PASS THROUGH THE CHAN GATE*

Commentary on a Discourse by Chan Master Huanglong Wuxin

Senior monks, a human birth is difficult to obtain. Buddhadharma is hard to get to hear. If you do not deliver this present human body in this lifetime, then, in what lifetime will you have a chance to deliver this human body? Do you people want to investigate Chan? Then you must let go. Let go of what? Let go of the four great elements and the five skandhas. You must let go of all your karmic consciousnesses accumulated through countless kalpas. Then, investigate exhaustively what is right under your own feet. What is the truth of it? Keep on pressing until your mind-flower suddenly gives forth brilliance, illuminating the world in the ten directions. Then, whatever your mind wishes, your hands will be able to obtain. You can then turn [the] earth into gold and turn the Yangtze River into ghee. Wouldn't this be a joyous thing in your life?

Do not involve yourself with reading words from books and discussing the path of Chan. The path of Chan is not present in books. Even if you read the whole Buddhist canon and the various classics from Chinese philosophers, since all of them will be idle words, none of them will be able to help you when you are facing death.

—from *Impetus to Pass through the Chan Gate*
by CHAN MASTER HUANGLONG WUXIN

Your Virtuous Karmic Potential

This morning when I came into the Chan Hall, there was a squirrel in here. When it saw me, it ran this way and that way, looked at me, and then it ran around in circles. When I opened the door to let it out, it stared at me then ran *away* from the open door. But when I closed the door, it ran *toward* the door. This is like you good people here—you have forgotten how you came in, and when the door is wide open, you don't know how to get out. [*Laughter*] Don't be like this squirrel. If you lose or stray from the method, as soon as you realize it, just pick it up again and continue. Don't be like that squirrel running around in circles, facing a dead end wherever it turns.

The purpose of this retreat is to become familiar with the huatou method, to understand how to use it, and then to apply it. I have already talked about the attitude and approaches one should take and shared with you some basic techniques. Since we are in the simplified space of a retreat center, it should be easy to use these methods. All you have to do is to listen, understand, and apply them. Unlike daily life where there are many distractions, practicing on retreat should be simple, so please try to grasp and use these methods.

Whether you will reach enlightenment depends on your virtuous karma, but for now your purpose is to hear Dharma, to become intimate with the process, and to let go of everything else. "To become intimate with the process" means getting closer and closer to the state of no-self; "to let go" means leaving vexations behind. How do you become intimate with no-self, and how do you let go of vexations? You use the tools and vehicles of Buddhadharma. However, to think that the tools and vehicles are themselves the goal is a mistake. In daily life, you use tools to accomplish certain tasks; Buddhadharma and practice should be looked upon in the same way. A correct understanding and a correct application of these tools and vehicles will take you to your goal.

What I call your virtuous karmic potential is difficult to explain; in fact, it is beyond explanation. But essentially, if you let go of all clinging to self-reference and attachment, then the resulting state of mind is the ripening of your virtuous karmic potential. What I have just given you is a summation of the purpose of Chan retreat: to become more and more intimate with the process of enlightenment. It is simultaneously letting go of vexations and suffering for the sake of yourself and others. How do you attain this goal of enlightenment? You use correct views and you use methods. The views give you a sense of direction; they guide you toward enlightenment, but they are only tools. Likewise the methods are tools that you use to stabilize and calm the mind. Once again, the tools are not the goal; they are used to reach the goal. Once you reach the goal, your karmic potential will have ripened.

The Difficulty of Obtaining a Human Birth

I will now comment on an excerpt by Chan Master Huanglong Wuxin (also known as Sixin Wuxin) from the text *Impetus to Pass through the Chan Gate*. It explains how one can practice to reach enlightenment, so let's look at the first two lines of the text:

> Senior monks, a human birth is difficult to obtain. Buddhadharma is hard to get to hear.

Senior monks were those who held the "upper" or high seats in the Chan Hall. The term is an honorific for monks who have upheld the full precepts for at least ten years. What is crucial in these lines is not whether the audience is an assembly of high-ranking monks, but the Buddhist idea about the preciousness of human life and the difficulty of encountering the Dharma. The difficulty of obtaining a human birth can be best understood in the context of the six realms of existence in samsara. One of the six realms is the realm of human beings. In the Buddhist view, only human beings have the opportunity to engage in Dharma practice and attain enlightenment.

How does one get reborn in this human realm? For one thing, cultivation of goodness is essential, but if one cultivates goodness in order to obtain merit [as opposed to virtue], they may be reborn in the heavenly realm of *devas* (gods) instead of the human realm. The problem is that devas cannot attain enlightenment and liberate themselves from samsara. As for those who engage in negative conduct, they may transmigrate to one of the lower realms—the animal, ghostly, or hell realms. The sixth realm is the realm of the titans, or jealous gods. From the human perspective these six realms of existence are not evenly populated. According to Buddhist belief the number of sentient beings existing in the human realm is by comparison very small.

Sentient beings reborn in the heavenly realm are completely absorbed in pleasure and bliss and therefore have no aspiration to practice Dharma. Even though their time in the heavenly realm is extremely long, ultimately it will come to an end. Nor do they have any sense of the final end until that time actually comes. When that final end comes, they must go alone without anyone taking notice. Why? Because all the other celestial beings are so wrapped up in their own pleasure, they do not notice someone missing. So the suffering of a heavenly being continues in another rebirth, because their karma has not been exhausted.

Unlike devas who experience only happiness, humans experience both suffering and pleasure. Perhaps for this reason people aspire toward freedom from anguish and lasting happiness. From the Buddhist point of view, what motivates someone to practice Dharma is the realization that suffering is a fundamental fact of existence. The more profound this understanding, the more their aspiration will be to attain liberation. The Buddha said, "Relinquish becoming and leave behind death." In other words, to terminate suffering, we need to transcend the cycle of birth and death. Having this aspiration, a person is said to have embarked on the path of renunciation. What if we got some animals to come to retreat, like that squirrel that was in here? Would they be able to engage in the practice? All of us here have obtained a human form and have engaged in practice, so we should see this as very rare and very precious.

Due to the acceptance in the East of the idea of reincarnation, for example, the Chinese have a saying, "It's all right if I die; eighteen years later I will be reborn as another person." This is not so funny in English, but this attitude of not regarding too preciously what one already has is common in the East. Perhaps modern people have a contrary idea, since there are so many human beings today. Maybe we should change Buddhist cosmology to suggest it is not that hard to become a human being. However, this would be wrong from the point of view of Dharma. Just because there are more people today, this does not mean that a human birth is easy to obtain. Other life forms such as animals may have exhausted their karma in that form and, due to their virtuous karma, are reborn as human beings. Another possibility is that sentient existence is not limited to this Earth; there are other galaxies, other dimensions beyond our knowledge; other systems of samsara may exist, and some sentient beings may even come here to be reborn.

What is the meaning of "Buddhadharma is hard to get to hear?" There are people who have never heard of Buddhadharma, and there are those who have heard but cannot accept it. Then there are those who have heard and accept the Dharma but have difficulty practicing it. For example, someone can be involved with Buddhadharma as a field of interest; they study it, teach it, even write books, but they don't use it to transform their own life. So, this line says that those who have actually heard the teachings, who accept, apply, and benefit from the teachings, are very rare. In this sense, Buddhadharma is hard to get to hear.

Still, there are some who have heard the teachings, accept them, and practice, but interpret them in their own way. They study the sutras, filtering the teachings through their own knowledge, thus transforming the teachings for themselves. After they absorb the teachings, they can give commentaries and share their understanding with others. But what they share can be quite different from true Buddhadharma.

So, this is another meaning of "Buddhadharma is hard to get to hear." Sometimes we don't really understand what we are hearing; we filter it through our own understanding. The point of coming to retreat is to actually hear and understand Dharma and to use it.

If you do not deliver this present human body in this lifetime, then, in what lifetime will you have a chance to deliver this human body?

Deriving genuine benefit from the Dharma entails sincere but difficult practice. We encounter hindrances when we become practitioners. For example, someone at this retreat says he wants to become a monk. His mother says, "When I am eighty years old, you can become a monk." At least she says, "You can become a monk"; it's just that she wants him to wait till she is eighty. Then, there are very clever people, probably smarter than the buddhas and certainly smarter than me, who say, "I have faith in the compassion of the buddhas, so there's no need for me to practice. At the threshold of my death, if they don't come to save me, that would mean buddhas are not compassionate." Some people point to Kshitigarbha Bodhisattva, who vowed to deliver all the sentient beings in the hell realm before attaining buddhahood for himself. So, they think, "I can just do what

I want. If I get reborn in the hell realm, Kshitigarbha Bodhisattva will be there to save me." These people are very clever indeed, to think they can go on with their life without practice and still be saved.

That's why Shakyamuni went through countless lives, practicing the Dharma, assuming different forms of existence before becoming the Buddha. And yet, his vows to practice were most effective as a human being, when he set his direction to the path of buddhahood. In realms other than the human realm, beings have neither the opportunity nor the capacity to practice. There are exceptions: an extremely small minority of heavenly beings can engage in some practice, but they cannot keep it up for too long. As a celestial being you would be experiencing so much pleasure that practice would be too difficult. What if we invite some *pretas,* "hungry ghosts," to come to retreat? They would listen to the Dharma and, being free of physical obstructions, they would quickly disappear. Why? Because their appearances are contingent on what is in their mind. As soon as their minds move, they will appear in the location that they thought of. You can look at that as either a blessing or as a curse. As for you, your mind can go anywhere in the world you want, but, for better or worse, your body will still be here. Some may think, "I would like to get out of this retreat." If they were hungry ghosts, instantly they would have been gone, but as human beings, when they open their eyes, they are still here. [*Laughter*]

Beyond Words and Language

The process of investigating Chan is difficult to explain because it is not about words, not about concepts, and is certainly not about knowledge. Free of these mental processes, what does it mean to investigate Chan? For lack of better words, it is to find yourself in a state of wonderment, of not knowing and yet urgently wanting to know. No one can tell you what it is; no one can give you the secret of "it." Even the buddhas have nothing to say about it.

What does it mean to investigate? This can only be known through personal experience, for it is not a simple matter of questioning. It is the process of entering into the huatou, experiencing fully this wanting to know, and this wonderment. When the doubt sensation is aroused, grows to a great doubt mass, and is completely shattered, only then will you know for yourself that there is no singular thing, that all things are just true suchness.

One mistake some practitioners make is to become entranced with the idea of true suchness as manifesting all things as perfect. This can lead to a kind of laziness with the attitude, "Yes, indeed, things are already perfect as they are. What is the need to practice, to contrive?" And when you ask them, "What is it?" they will answer, "It is as it is." When you question further, they might respond, "What else do you want from me? Things are such as they are. If you don't believe me, here, I'll take off my clothes to show you." [*Laughter*] This can happen to practitioners who are lazy.

Then there are those who have read widely and have some understanding of the Chan lineage masters and have grasped the essential teaching of nonattachment. To them, all the words they have read point to this: do not attach to anything. And so, if you ask, "How is your practice?" they might reply, "When am I *not* practicing?" When you ask them, "What insights have you gained?" they might say, "If I meet the Buddha, I will kill him, and if Mara appears, I will also kill him. What other kind of insights do you want?" This is an example of a mistaken view of what nonattachment means.

There is a story about the fourth patriarch of Chan, Daoxin (580–651), that illustrates a more subtle kind of attachment. When Daoxin visited a mountain monastery, he met a very diligent monk named Niutou Farong (594–657). On one occasion, learning that the younger monk was in the habit of meditating on a certain rock, Daoxin wrote on the rock the Chinese character for buddha (*fo*). When Farong saw the word "buddha" written on the rock, he hesitated to sit on it. Upon seeing that, Daoxin remarked to Farong, "So, you still have *that* left in you?" When Farong heard that, his mind-ground suddenly opened up and he became enlightened.

Chan stories like this have contributed to practitioners straying off the path, especially clever ones: "Oh! So the essence of the story must be that the Buddha is within all of us. That means we don't have to practice, we just don't attach to anything. No need to be attached to the word 'buddha' either." So, misguided people, based on such understanding, harm their wisdom life. In fact, you could say they put to death their own wisdom life, so they are unable to make progress. Similarly, all of you can say to each other, "Going to Chan retreat?" Most of what we do is sitting meditation, so you can say to each other, "Oh, we still have *this* left." But in fact, without methods, how can one practice? So, clinging to such a notion of nonattachment, they put to death their own potential. In Chan we call this "dying at the threshold of spoken words." "Spoken words" refers to the gong'an, and "dying at the threshold of spoken words" is becoming stuck on those words and stories.

Now, both of these types of people do not know the meaning of investigating Chan, let alone actually practicing Chan. So what is the first type?

Students: Lazy.

Sheng Yen: And what is the second type?

Students: Clever.

Sheng Yen: Who then are the people who are truly investigating Chan? We shall see. They better be neither lazy nor clever. [*Laughter*]

Do you people want to investigate Chan? Then you must let go.

As the text points out, true Chan adepts let go of clinging to self. If someone thinks, "Under the heaven, I am the most important person in the world," you would say this person indulges in self-aggrandizement and arrogance. Such a person might have difficulty letting go of self-centeredness. Now, let me ask: what about those who have low self-esteem and pity themselves, who lack faith? "I'm a miserable person, I can't practice." Do you think there's ego there? We may regard people who think that they have heavy karma and can't practice Dharma as being without ego. In fact, this kind of negative self-esteem is akin to those who are very proud and arrogant. Both types show signs of strong self-attachment.

It is natural for famous people to be arrogant and proud, but people who constantly filter their experience through their low self-esteem, who appear to be humble, also have strong self-attachment. Furthermore, the shell of their attachment is as solid as the shell of the arrogant people at the other end of the pole. These two kinds of people at opposite extremes have the strongest sense of ego, and it is very difficult for them to practice Chan. It is those who neither think of themselves as important nor as pitiable, who see things in a normal perspective, who can best practice Chan: "Yes, I have my share of vexations, but I am also able to practice Chan." I hope you all belong to this last category. People like this see themselves in correct relation to others and to things, and therefore recognize they need to practice diligently. Practice what? Letting go of vexations and putting down self-centeredness.

Then there are those practitioners who put up a facade. Externally they are humble, but they do not feel that way inside. They are introverted with strong self-attachment. Such people also do not cultivate relations with others, tend to hide things, and keep a closed mind, as if unwilling to share their secrets. Even till their bones burn to ashes, they will forever hold their secret, fearing to lose their sense of security or lose face. Another type of practitioner is one whose self-centeredness is equally strong, but is also very extroverted. Instead of hiding, they want to open themselves up to everyone, anytime. They will share their views with other people but really do not care whether others are listening: "You know, I have this problem, and this and that and that and that," and they'll do this in situations where it is really uncalled for. So there is a strong sense of self there. While Chan practitioners have an openness of mind, they relate to others appropriately, without a need to tell everyone about themselves.

Mind and Body: Two Aspects of Self

Master Huanglong's text continues to say:

> Let go of what? Let go of the four great elements and the five skandhas. You must let go of all your karmic consciousnesses accumulated through countless kalpas.

If we can let go of the four elements, the five *skandhas*, and karmic consciousnesses, then this is letting go of self. The four elements—earth, water, fire, and wind—make up our physical body, which we identify as part of our self. The five skandhas, or aggregates, are the factors that make up what we are as human beings. They are form, sensation, perception, volition, and consciousness. Form is the physical aggregate, and includes the four elements. The remaining four skandhas are mental in nature and together govern the workings of the mind, the second aspect of our sense of self. The mind's identification with the body and its interactions with the environment result in our sense of self. The mind itself is a process of *sensing, perceiving,* and *acting* upon perceptions (the volition factor), leading to awareness, or *consciousness.* These four mental processes are a result of mutual interactions of the body with all its sense faculties coming in contact with phenomena. In this manner our mind comes into being, experiences phenomena, and attaches to those experiences as a sense of self.

In the *Sutra of Complete Enlightenment* there are these sentences: "[We] falsely attach to the four elements as the characteristics of the body, and in delusion we take the impressions of six sense faculties as our mind." It is not even the six sense faculties but the impressions, shadows if you will, of the workings of the senses that we take as mind. As Master Huanglong points out, the sense of self essentially comes from the two aspects of body and mind. I will not go into detail about the four phases of the working of mind—sensation, perception, volition, and consciousness. All we need to know now is that we identify these four skandhas, together with the body—the skandha of form—as our self.

For most people, the four elements and the five skandhas are just abstractions; they can easily recite them if asked, but such notions have nothing to do with their actual being. They can even say, "Oh, the four elements and five skandhas? They're empty." But their own body they do not see as empty. If you want to practice Chan, I would advise you not to look at your body as "me" or "my." Rather, look upon the body as a tool for practice. If you see your body as "my body," you may want to cherish it too much. Another extreme is to treat your body very badly. Both of these are wrong attitudes. Just simply, see your body as a tool to cultivate the Dharma.

What is the meaning then of the five skandhas? They are also tools that we use. Well, to whom do they belong? They don't belong to me. The five skandhas belong to the five skandhas; they are just the five skandhas, and we use them to practice. When we can do this, the skandhas will no longer be that solid and firm, and our self-centeredness will decrease. We can finally let go of the karmic consciousness accumulated through countless aeons.

Karmic Consciousness

"Karmic consciousness" is a technical Buddhist term that comes from, in particular, the treatise called *The Awakening of Mahayana Faith*, attributed to the Indian sage Ashvaghosha. The term refers to the source of our cyclic existence as well as our emotional afflictions, and it specifically refers to our repository of karmic potential or "seeds" that we carry from one life to another. The technical term for this is *alayavijnana*, or "storehouse consciousness." All you have to know now is that karmic consciousness is the source of our cyclic existence in samsara (birth and death) and the source of our afflictions. On the positive side, this very karmic consciousness contains the seeds, or potential, for wisdom and compassion to freely function as an aspect of *tathagatagarbha*, the seminal buddha-nature we all have. All the vows and acts of the buddhas are contained in tathagatagarbha as potential. The difference is that the buddhas are free from karmic impressions, yet are able to use this kind of consciousness on the level of phenomena to respond to sentient beings. So, there is the potential to transform alayavijnana to the free function of wisdom and compassion, the fulfillment of vows, and pure conduct. So, whether we call it alayavijnana or tathagatagarbha, both refer to this karmic consciousness.

When buddhas manifest in samsara, they use this kind of consciousness while remaining free of attachments and vexations. So, on the one hand we have sentient beings whose karmic consciousness is a source of their continual rounds of birth and death as well as continued vexation. On the other hand we have the buddhas freely using this quality of consciousness to respond to sentient beings. Whether we call the illusory nature of consciousness alayavijnana or tathagatagarbha, it does not refer to true suchness, *tathata*, which is not a function. True suchness is motionless and ever unmoving, but in the phenomenal world the buddhas appear as illusory transformations to deliver sentient beings, while being free of the delusions of ordinary sentient beings.

How do all these ideas relate to Chan? Huanglong tells us to let go of all of our karmic consciousnesses. The plural form used here refers to both karmic consciousness as well as tathagatagarbha. Karmic consciousness is the aspect that constantly generates vexations, so we should definitely let go of that. What about the free functions of wisdom and compassion, which Dharma seekers aspire to? That mentality should also be let go of. So, along with karmic consciousness, Chan practitioners should not cling to notions about tathagatagarbha, the functioning of wisdom.

If we cannot let go of body and mind, at the very least we should relax and try to conduct our affairs in a relaxed manner. Some practitioners have very scattered minds and lots of discursive thoughts. So they may say, "I cannot embarrass myself by showing how scattered I am, but at least I can try to sit very still." In this manner they start this inner conflict of forcing themselves to sit well. This is like a general with a facade of arrogance but who is insecure inside. Then there are the practitioners with a tourist's mentality. They come here not so much to practice as to watch other people practice. They have heard that a Chan retreat can be very difficult but that it can also be very wonderful, so they want to find out for themselves. It is not really for their own experience but to see what it is like to go on a Chan retreat: "What are the people doing?" They refuse to involve themselves in the practice, much less plunge into it. This is another mistake. For the rest of us, we need to engage the practice in a down-to-earth manner, without struggling with ourselves, without a tourist's mentality of sightseeing, but really sincerely using the method to the best of our ability. When we can do this, we will be able to subdue this mind of vexations and integrate the Dharma into our being.

Shattering the Great Doubt

We have spoken about the need for practitioners to let go of the four elements and the five skandhas, as well as our karmic consciousnesses. The four elements and five skandhas comprise the body and mind. By "karmic consciousnesses," we mean the mind of vexation as well as the mind of an eventual buddha. We need to let go of the mind that wants to escape vexations as well as the mind that seeks merit and virtue. This is because the more we want to be rid of our vexations, the more they will flourish; the more we seek after merit, the further bodhi will recede. Therefore, we must let go of everything.

The Dharma is indeed wondrous yet very difficult to understand. This is because from the point of view of Buddhadharma, most people's view of the world is upside-down. With topsy-turvy habits of thinking, reflecting, and speaking, how can an afflicted mind know correct Buddhadharma? How can that person investigate Chan? From the point of view of Dharma, all our acquired worldly knowledge is, as the *Heart Sutra* says, confused imaginings. With this upside-down mind-set, trying to filter the Dharma through our habitual ways of thinking is very difficult. That is why Huanglong says, "Buddhadharma is hard to get to hear." However, if people recognize that their views are actually upside-down, perhaps they may have a chance of practicing Chan and grasping Buddhadharma. Otherwise, continuing their own ways, acquiring worldly knowledge and upside-down views of reality, the Dharma will be far away.

The reason it may be difficult to believe that most people's thinking is inverted is because it is so widespread. If you point out to someone that from the view of Dharma their thinking is incorrect, they might say, "Everyone else thinks like me, so how can I be upside-down?" They cannot recognize it and cannot accept the Buddha's ideas. Except when they are out hunting for food, bats literally spend their lives hanging upside down. If everyone else is upside-down, that condition will seem normal. They can't recognize it, so they will doubt what the Buddha says. So many people are like bats living with an upside-down view of the world.

So, today, I say we must also let go of inverted, upside-down views. What are some upside-down views? Clinging to karmic consciousness, constant self-referencing, wanting things, wanting to acquire Dharma, and yearning for enlightenment. But aren't you here to acquire Dharma and enlightenment? Didn't you come to relinquish your vexations, realizing you have suffering in your life? You may think, "Yes, I have a lot of suffering. I have vexations. I want to get rid of vexations. I want to reach enlightenment. I want to become a buddha. I want to be reborn in the Pure Land." Everything is "I," "I," "me," "me." These are all inverted views, and with these perspectives, one creates more suffering. We call this the "first ultimate truth," which is that all such mind-sets create more karma and more suffering. And this is also what Huanglong means by "karmic consciousness."

If you can recognize, "Yes, my views are deluded; the way I think, my acquired knowledge is upside-down," then you can accept and practice Dharma. But then again, some people may soon enough have doubts. The first day, they may listen and think, "Yes, I agree," and tomorrow, they will say, "Prove it to me. Why does Dharma say this? Doesn't Buddhadharma say this and that?" This habit is also a manifestation of karmic consciousness. So, you must let go of these doubts too. Generally speaking, you must let go of the mind-set of wanting to get rid of something and wanting to get something; you must put aside both wanting to be rid of suffering and wanting to get enlightened. Without rejecting or seeking, just hold on dearly to your huatou; glue yourself to it and continue to ask.

Prior to becoming enlightened, Mazu Daoyi (709–788) was a very diligent practitioner who meditated all day and all night. One day, while he was deep in meditation, Master Nanyue Huairang (677–744) approached Mazu and asked him why he was sitting so diligently. When Mazu replied that he was sitting in order to become a buddha, Huairang picked up a brick and sat next to Mazu and started to polish the brick. Puzzled at this behavior, Mazu asked Huairang why he was polishing the brick. Master Huairang answered that he was making a mirror. Mazu said, "But, Master, you cannot make a mirror by polishing a brick!" Huairang replied, "And you can't become a buddha by sitting in meditation." Mazu asked,

"Then what is the correct way?" Huairang replied, "If the cart isn't moving, do you whip the cart or the ox?"

This is not to say that meditation is not useful. The point is that trying to become enlightened through meditation is precisely the karmic consciousness of a seeking mind. When we are seeking, there is also rejecting, and when we seek and reject, we create vexations. That very seeking mind—sitting in meditation hoping to become a buddha—was Mazu's obstacle to enlightenment. But when Mazu realized that his attachment to the idea of buddhahood was an obstruction, he became enlightened.

Then, investigate exhaustively what is right under your own feet.

"Investigate exhaustively" means investigating your huatou, applying your method to discover what is right under your own feet. "What is right under your own feet" is a Chan expression for the very roots of your existence. You must plunge your whole being into the huatou; you must exhaustively continue to question. Only then will you expose the roots of your existence, which are none other than your afflictions, your attachments, and your deeply embedded sense of self. To truly investigate Chan, you must use the huatou to uproot this thick, tall tree that is firmly planted in the mind. To uproot this tree of karmic consciousness, you must dig from the roots up. However deep the roots may extend, that's how deep you must go. Once you have uprooted this tree, you can hurl it into vast, empty space and allow it to dissolve.

People do not recognize the roots of their vexations, the source of their self-clinging. All they know is, "I like this, I don't like that. I want this, I don't want that." So, all day long they drown in these mental states. If you ask them, "What is the root, the very source, of these vexations?" they have no idea. "What is the origin of self-clinging?" "I don't know." If you really press, they may say, "My parents are my roots." Think about this: a father and a mother are only the roots of your physical being; as for the roots of your vexation and self-clinging, they are beyond physical.

If we do not know of the root of our vexations, how will we ever know how deep they are? Typically, we do not know; all we know is what we face in the external environment. Our mind is geared toward the outside: "I don't like this, I don't like that." For example, you came to retreat voluntarily to be isolated for seven days, and that's not all: For seven days your legs have to fold in a certain way, causing you physical discomfort, pain, distress, even anguish. Moreover, vexations that you never thought you had flourish. But that's all to the good. Most people will blame others for their own vexations: "I have finally discovered the source of my vexations. It's *him*." Who is this "him"? It's that old monk, who put up this retreat center: "What kind of hell is this place, isolating people in silence, having to listen to snoring all night long! [*Laughter*] And during the day, what's wrong with a little chat between friends? Finally, I've discovered the source of my vexations. It is that old monk." But actually, the source of vexations does not come from anything outside. You have brought them with you, not only to this retreat; you have brought them with you from countless lifetimes in the past. You have accumulated many seeds of suffering, and now in this life, due to causes and conditions, they manifest before you, and, clouded by delusion, you do not see this. What we see is others causing us suffering, anxiety, and trouble.

Therefore, your task is to dig up the roots of vexation and examine them. But then again, those who are clever, smart devils will ask themselves questions like, "What's at the root of huatou itself?" And so they start having doubts; not the genuine doubt of Chan, but skeptical doubt, doubting what I say, doubting the Dharma. This is an obstacle to practicing Chan. Therefore, it is very hard for clever people to practice Chan. But it is those simpler types who will think, "I must take to heart Shifu's words and investigate this huatou sincerely, so I will ask, 'What is *wu*?'" Simple people know how to practice Chan directly, while the smart ones use their brains to figure out things. As a result, they cannot gain access to their true being. Ever since I was young, I was quite dim-witted, and for this reason I have come to understand just a little bit of what Chan is about.

> What is the truth of it? Keep on pressing until your mind-flower suddenly gives forth brilliance, illuminating the world in the ten directions.

"What is the truth of it?" describes the questioning state of mind: "What is it? What is it? What is the root of my own existence? What is the root of vexations, of self-clinging?" Wanting deeply to know the truth—this is the doubt sensation that arises when we investigate Chan. When genuine doubt sensation arises, there is a feeling of deeply wanting to know the truth. When we continue to press on with the huatou, then it is possible for the doubt sensation to evolve into the great doubt mass. When this great mass of doubt engulfs you, you have become one with the doubt. You have dealt yourself into this great doubt mass that engulfs your whole being as well as your whole world.

These lines actually describe three stages: The question, "What is the truth of it?" describes the doubt sensation arising in the mind of the practitioner. Pressing on, one will eventually give rise to what is called the great doubt mass, or the great ball of doubt. After that, if conditions are ripe, a catalytic event or stimulus may cause the great doubt mass to shatter, or dissolve. Depending on the strength of one's doubt, self-centeredness is abandoned and they may experience awakening.

The Three Stages of Doubt

To summarize, there are three stages in the development and resolution of Chan doubt: first, *giving rise to the doubt sensation;* second, *generating the great doubt mass;* and third, *shattering the great doubt mass.* To give rise to doubt, it is crucial to have faith: you believe firmly in your own buddha-nature, and you believe firmly that the huatou will lead you to awakening to buddha-nature. When you have established this faith, the doubt can then arise. How does it arise? It arises by your continually asking the huatou. For example, you may be asking, asking, and asking the huatou. Meanwhile, in the back of your mind, there is the intention of wanting to know, the urge, the thirst of wanting to find the answer that you truly believe the huatou will reveal. So along with asking, you continue to want to know and you nourish that intention. And when that intention genuinely, spontaneously arises by itself, this thirst of wanting to know the answer is the doubt sensation.

If you press on with the huatou but the doubt sensation does not arise, that is called "repeating." That is because, although you continue to ask the huatou, your asking is really not consonant with the huatou method. In that sense, your asking is more akin to reciting the Buddha's name or reciting a mantra. This can be useful for calming the mind, but this repetitive practice is not the true function of the huatou method. When you can ask the huatou with faith and conviction, the doubt sensation will arise.

When you continue to press on and the doubt sensation becomes stronger, it is possible for the doubt sensation to evolve into a great doubt mass. This great mass of doubt is a continuation of the strong feeling of wanting to know the answer to your huatou, with the difference that it now engulfs your whole mind. At such a time, the words of the huatou may not persist in your mind. The words, "What is *wu?*" can vanish, leaving you with only this thirst, this wanting to know. At that time, this sheer momentum of wanting to know, wanting to know—"What is it? What is it?"—engulfs your whole being. You are now *inside* the huatou.

How does it feel to be inside a huatou? On the one hand, it is a sense of unending wonderment, wanting to know. On the other hand, since it engulfs you, your whole world, your whole being, it is a suffocating feeling. It is not that your mind is vexed; rather, this questioning, this strong urge, is a kind of weight on your mind. Furthermore, this strong urge cannot be stopped and continues of its own accord. So, in that sense, it is a kind of suffocating feeling hovering over you, holding you down, and you cannot break through. And still, you do not know the answer to your huatou. The feeling of the great doubt mass can be likened to a chick trying to poke through its shell but is not there yet, still in darkness, not seeing the light. This ball of doubt hovers over you and brings a sense of burden, a pressing feeling. You press on, and when that doubt finally shatters, you experience awakening to insight, and your "mind-flower suddenly gives forth brilliance, illuminating the world in the ten directions."

Sometimes the doubt does not build to the point of shattering, but rather, the accumulated energy dissipates; energy leaks out, as if there were a hole in your ball of doubt. The cause can be one of two things: First, your body is not robust enough to carry you through resolving this doubt mass, and you become fatigued. Secondly, and more crucially, the doubt mass cannot grow because you lack faith either in the method or in yourself, or both. While you are engulfed in this doubt, you may begin to waver: "Is this it? Should I go on?" As soon as such a thought occurs, it can cause "leakage" of that energy, and the great doubt mass will begin to lose strength. That turn of events will not take you through to a resolution of the huatou.

The Great Doubt in Daily Life

By contrast, when practicing huatou in daily life, this great mass of doubt manifests in a more subtle but steady manner. It does not have the same intensity as when you dedicate yourself to it for an extended period, as on retreat. In daily life, the great doubt mass is more like something in your throat that you can neither swallow nor spit out. This kind of doubt sensation is not turbulent and energetic; rather it is steady and ongoing, underlying your daily activities. You can still cope, deal with work, take up responsibilities, but there's just this one single question that's always in the back of your mind, working away patiently.

Even though it occurs in daily life, when conditions are right, it is also possible for that doubt mass to shatter and lead to an awakening. You may be walking down the street and a bird shits on your head, and at that time your doubt mass is shattered. You are filled with joy: "Finally, I know *wu*!" Has your discovery of *wu* anything to do with bird shit? Not a single thing. The point is that when you are in the midst of the great doubt mass and your mind is ripe, any occurrence can be a catalyst to clear away vexations and illuminate the mind with wisdom. This is the doubt mass and the shattering of it in daily circumstances. The case where the great doubt mass overwhelms and engulfs you occurs mainly in a setting where you are dedicated to practice over a long period, like on retreat.

Now that you have learned about how the shattering of the great doubt mass can result in the dropping away of the self, you may go home thinking you know something about it. Unless you directly experience the shattering of the great doubt mass yourself, what you have learned is just intellectual knowledge. Although it is useful for your own practice, until you experience the great doubt mass yourself, to speak about these ideas as genuinely yours is vexation.

At the Threshold of Hell

With retreat nearly ending, how many of you are thinking of leaving? None? How many think that the last several days have gone by in a flash? Ah! Thank you. Probably none of you have been to hell [in a previous life], but how many feel that the retreat has brought you to the threshold of hell? [*Laughter*] Only one? [*Referring to respondent*] You have been on retreat three times, so this is your third trip to hell? [*Laughter*] According to scripture, Kshitigarbha Bodhisattva said, "If I don't enter the hell realm to help sentient beings there, who will?" So, like Kshitigarbha, you can say, "If I don't enter hell, then who will?" [*Laughter*] There's a Chinese saying, "There are many roads to heaven, yet we do not take them." On the other hand, there is no gate to hell, yet everyone wants to rush in. Time in heaven goes by very quickly, but time in hell is very long.

> Then, whatever your mind wishes, your hands will be able to obtain. You can then turn [the] earth into gold and turn the Yangtze River into ghee. Wouldn't this be a joyous thing in your life?

Transforming the great earth into gold, the rivers into ghee is actually a metaphor for the freedom of mind that one experiences upon realizing wisdom. Huanglong is saying that the state of mind after enlightenment is one of mastery, of finally being at ease, and having the power to metaphorically transform the world at will. Not only have you obtained human life and heard the Dharma, but you have made full use of this precious human life. Your life has been most meaningful, not a waste, and isn't it wonderful to be enlightened?

This is a very tempting and alluring depiction of enlightenment, isn't it? Today, I drove to the city, and while there Guogu [the translator] went into a deli looking for vegetarian soup but they did not have any. No lunch for us. Was this because we are not enlightened? [*Laughter*] Going into the city was fine because we had the windows open, but coming back was like being inside a rice cooker. So I asked Guogu to turn on the air conditioner. "It's not working," he said. So, Guogu eventually took off his robe, and he wanted to take off another piece of clothing but hesitated. Then, I myself took off my robe. And I said, "If I had supernatural power, I could make the air conditioner work." [*Laughter*]

Chan is a down-to-earth, humanistic approach that focuses on the reality of being human and downplays supernatural powers, extrasensory perceptions, and so on. Chan masters not only refuse to use supernatural powers, they rebuke those who do. The focus in Chan is to release the mind from obstructions, to let go of clinging and grasping, and to realize the free flowing of enlightened wisdom. Supernatural powers are limited and unreliable. They can only help certain people, not everyone. More important, the use of supernatural powers cannot undo past karma. If using supernatural power conflicts with one's karma, this can increase the retribution that will come due in the future. It may be possible to use supernatural powers to sidetrack or delay retribution, but sooner or later, retribution will come due and perhaps with interest. By sharp contrast, the application of wisdom can help resolve karmic retribution in an effective and thorough way. For this reason Chan downplays supernatural abilities.

Huanglong's description of the great earth as gold and the rivers as ghee expresses his own experience of something that is really ineffable. A person who is enlightened, whose mind is unobstructed and free, would see an ordinary world of mountains and rivers as nourishing elements for sentient beings. Sentient beings could not live without water, and living beings would not be possible without the earth. Whether these transformations really happened is not the issue.

In Chan lore there was an eccentric monk and poet named "Cold Mountain," Hanshan (ca. 730–ca. 850), whose name derives from the name of the mountain he lived on, Cold Mountain. (This Hanshan is different than the Hanshan Deqing whose text we looked at in the first chapter of part 2.) In one of his poems he describes the clouds as his blanket, the rocks as his pillows, the mountain itself as his bed, and the river as his bathtub. The mountain where he stayed was cold and barren and not so rich in forestry. He was so poor he didn't even have proper clothes. Running around in the woods without pants, he was ridiculed, but he laughed, saying, "It is you who are destitute, whereas I, Cold Mountain, the whole world belongs to me."

Actually, Hanshan did not stay at Cold Mountain all the time. He sojourned to many places and did not own a single thing. Actually the whole earth was his bed; wherever he went, he felt very natural and at ease, even though no one recognized him. In the time of the Buddha, mendicant monks owned only their robe and an alms bowl, yet they felt content and at ease. There's a saying, "Walk under the heaven with one bowl and the food of a thousand households is yours." For these mendicant monks there was no worrying about food or dwellings. When they sat under a tree, for that moment it was their home. In that part of India the thick forests provided shelter from rain and the elements, so they could remain there at will. Once the rain passed, they could move on. Even though they didn't own anything, they felt at ease and content with a deep sense of security. What they had was freedom of mind, and this is most important. Buddhism offers people freedom of mind: freedom in oneself as well as freedom for others. Once the mind is free, then the whole world transforms. There's no need to travel to other places such as the Pure Land.

Once when the Buddha was on one of his rounds of begging, he came across a farmer who was reluctant to give him any food. Thinking that the Buddha was just another *shramana,* a mendicant, he said, "You don't work; all you know is how to beg for food, whereas I work very diligently. I cultivate my field and crops. If you want food, you can cultivate these fields yourself." The Buddha, upon hearing this, said, "Yes, indeed you work hard to cultivate your fields. I, too, cultivate fields." The farmer asked, "What kind of field do you cultivate?" The Buddha replied, "I do not cultivate a field of soil; I cultivate the field of mind, not only my mind but the minds of all sentient beings. Through expedient means I plant seeds and cultivate the mind-ground of sentient beings. Eventually the fields will also blossom and produce crops." So, upon hearing this teaching, the farmer was filled with great faith and sincerely offered food to the Buddha. The point is that the function of the Dharma is to encourage people to cultivate freedom of the mind. For example, a shramana, which is nowadays a monk or nun, should not have to worry about food; in fact, they also should not have to worry about clothing, shelter, and so on. What they really should focus on is whether their minds are in accordance with Buddhadharma, whether they have given rise to bodhichitta, and whether they have a mind of renunciation. For lay practitioners, while earning a livelihood, they should also arouse bodhichitta and practice renunciation.

Bodhichitta is compassion, the mind-set of offering oneself for the benefit of others; renunciation is the wisdom that penetrates vexations and abandons suffering. When one has compassion on the one hand and wisdom on the other, those who know you will cherish you as a friend. You will be able to live a way of life that's sufficient. So, with bodhichitta and renunciation one has the mind-set of being on the path. This prompts me to recall my dissertation advisor at Rissho University in Japan. One time I was quite destitute and did not have the means to continue my education, and he said something to me that made a lasting impression. He said, "When the mind is set on food and clothing, there is no mind for the way, but when the mind is set on the way, food and clothing will be sufficient." This inspired me at the time, and I personally testify to the truth of this observation.

So, did any of you come here expecting to find gold and ghee? At the end of the retreat I gave in Berlin, I told them I had given each one of them ten tons of gold that they should slowly digest. They were very happy with that. [Laughter] One person commented, however, "So much gold! What shall I do with it?" Indeed, having so much gold can be a problem. What would you do if the whole earth turned to gold? Using your reasoning mind, you may think, "That would be a big problem—there'd be nothing to eat." Fortunately, Huanglong tells us we will have ghee to eat. [*Laughter*]

Getting back to the text, how can we transform ourselves and the world? We must first let go of self-centeredness, resentment, jealousy, and arrogance. When we let go of all self-clinging, then the world, the corresponding world, will also change. Earth will turn to gold; the rivers will turn to ghee, and this describes the state of freedom, unobstructed by anything.

Master Huanglong's text continues:

Do not involve yourself with reading words from books and discussing the path of Chan. The path of Chan is not present in books. Even if you read the whole Buddhist canon and the various classics from Chinese philosophers, since all of them will be idle words, none of them will be able to help you when you are facing death.

Huanglong clearly says that Chan cannot be practiced through words and books. Even if you read the whole Buddhist canon and the Chinese classics, it will not be useful to you at the threshold of death. "Facing death" also refers to our future beyond this particular death. Where will we be reborn? Do we know our destiny? Do not misunderstand: this passage does *not* mean that the sutras, commentaries, and discourse records are useless. The point is that relying only on words is a wrong way to practice—like eating crumbs left on the table by other people. How nourishing can that be?

There was a man who attended one of my retreats, and whenever I gave a Dharma talk, he would add a few words to my commentary. Afterward, I asked him, "How much Dharma do you know?" Very freely and spontaneously he uttered some enlightened-sounding words. I said, "Well, you are well-read." He replied, "Yes, in fact, all the famous Chan texts, such as *The Five Lamps Merging at the Source* and *The Transmission of the Lamp,* I have read extensively. You are probably not as familiar as I am with these texts." And he stood there smiling at me. So, I said, "Yes, you're very familiar with these texts, but even a parrot can recite words." The reason I said that was because this fellow's understanding was intellectual and not based on actual realization.

The scriptures and the discourse records of the Buddha and the Chan masters point to a reality that they testify to; they inspire us to personally experience the teachings in them, and that is the essential truth. The other day I also urged all of you to personally experience my words and not to go around selling Dharma after the retreat. What is most important is for us to use these teachings in our lives, to actually experience them.

I sincerely advise you to give up distracting thoughts and emotional ups and downs. Do not involve yourself in trivia. For the remaining time, please give rise to vows, so as to give yourself a direction, to urge yourself on. Give rise to great compassion as the motivation for practice. Stick to your method every minute, from one instant to the next. Rest your mind on the method, and vow not to go astray. Free yourself from the mind's inner chattering. In this simplified space of a retreat, you can become friends with the method and learn the correct attitudes and approach to practice. Only by making vows will you be able to use what you have learned in the complex situation of daily life. Only then will you recognize vexations as they arise. In the midst of daily life you may not recognize the more subtle vexations, but coarser ups and downs and selfish clinging you will definitely recognize right away. Your ability to do that depends on your familiarity with this method of cultivation. Otherwise, you will continue to create karma without even recognizing it. So, make vows, and stay with the method—hold on dearly to these two principles, and integrate them into your being.

The Sword of Wisdom

In depictions of Manjushri Bodhisattva, he is often shown holding in his right hand the double-edged sword of wisdom. As the embodiment of Buddhist wisdom, Manjushri is said to use this sword to cut off ignorance and attachment. Similarly, the practice of huatou is often described as wielding the diamond-cutting sword of wisdom. Those not adept at the practice will identify the huatou with this, that, and everything, but true adepts will use the method to cut through delusions inside, outside, and in between. I had a student who was practicing huatou, and I pointed to a bench and asked him, "What is it?" He replied, "*Wu.*" This represents a non-Buddhist view in which the goal is to experience everything as one. Someone who experiences this kind of oneness will tend to see everything as manifestations of a deity, creator, or grand designer. As such, everything has this "it" which points to God, an almighty creator. In this view, all things are manifestations of this grand designer.

Therefore, practicing huatou in order to realize oneness is a mistake if that means clinging to *wu.* Genuine practice means using the huatou as a sword to cut off and put aside whatever manifests before you. When you let go of all manner of clinging, that is the correct way to use the huatou. Nonattachment itself is the correct way to practice. If someone has difficulty using huatou, that is often due to either lack of faith in the method or to inadequate energy. If a person has confidence in the method but the body cannot undergo the rigor, that person will not practice effectively. For example, one of you was earnest to try the method after hearing all the talk and knowing that everyone was doing it. I had no heart to tell him, "You are too old for this practice." Even when practicing following the breath, he falls asleep, and with breath counting, he has so much chatter in his mind. Even though he believes in the method, he has insufficient physical and mental energy to use it well. Finally, he has been doing a lot of volunteer work, so there is the danger that practicing huatou will exhaust him. I don't want him to give up the practice because of that.

However, it is possible for even a person with limited energy to use the method occasionally in daily life. When you are having problems and when others see your vexation, at that time you can bring forth the huatou and ask, "What is *wu*?" You can do this whenever you confront difficulties or vexations, and perhaps redirect your vexations to gradually calm down. You can also pick up the huatou when you are tired yet cannot sleep because your mind is churning. You can ask, "What is *wu*?" while lying in bed. The next morning, when you wake up, you may wonder, "Wasn't I supposed to be investigating *wu*? What happened?" And you can pick it up again. Do not be discouraged if your body is not strong enough or if your mind is too scattered. You can still use this approach in daily life. Pick up the huatou occasionally and ask the question, and perhaps one day, at eighty, you may wake up and say, "Aha!" [*Laughter*] Perhaps it won't take you that long. The point is that it will not work in daily life if you haphazardly pick up *wu*; it will only work if you steadily use this method when you encounter vexations. The practice will eventually mature and your wife will be able to testify to your *wu*. One day, she will tell you, "This *wu* that you've been using, it's working—you've changed." [*Laughter*]

If you are using the Silent Illumination practice and are using it well, or if you are contemplating the breath or any other method, you can once in a while pick up this huatou and use it in your life. But remember, occasional practice of huatou in daily life is very different from dedicated practice over an extended period. Daily-life practice of huatou, as you recall, is not that fierce, and you only occasionally pick it up. If you tried to practice it intensely in daily life, it would become more of a distraction than help. Your interactions with other people will also be impeded because you may exhibit mental states that they may see as neurotic or strange.

I want to now summarize what I have been saying. First we should place equal weight on concepts and methods. Second, we need faith in the method and confidence in our ability to practice. Third, we need to give rise to bodhichitta and renunciation. In terms of specific views, I have spoken about impermanence again and again. And I have spoken of impermanence in relation to selflessness. In relation to selflessness, I referred to the Middle Way, which says that due to conditioned arising, phenomena are empty of self-nature. In terms of the method, I focused on the teaching of huatou, how to use it, including the stages and direct contemplation. Direct contemplation should not be used in the Chan Hall; it is more of an auxiliary, supporting practice to your main method while outdoors.

Diligence

I have already mentioned the importance of humility, repentance, and diligence. Right now I want to elaborate on diligence. Without diligence we can lose the practice entirely, or we end up practicing only sporadically. No one deliberately wants to be lazy. However, people encounter situations where they feel hopeless and cannot summon the energy to be diligent. Some examples include failing to get what we want, having to give up something we cherish, falling behind in a competitive situation, and so on. These are different kinds of suffering people experience, but unless we accept the obligations that come with existence, we will not be able to practice well. Without experiencing suffering, people would not be motivated to practice. Experiencing the anguish of life should give rise to greater diligence, not less. But when we accept responsibility for our life and become diligent, our mind becomes bright and energetic, and confidence will spontaneously arise.

Another reason we lack diligence is because our understanding of birth and death is shallow, even though this concerns our own ultimate death. Unless we have a very personal experience of death, it is difficult to give rise to genuine diligence. If we have been on the threshold of death and survived, such an experience will urge us to live life with greater meaning. Similarly, witnessing the death of someone close can also urge us not to wait to acquire the skills for helping others.

In one of the sutras, the Buddha tells a story about a man who was being chased by four bandits who wanted his belongings and his life. As he was running, he came across a well and thought it would be a good place to hide. On the top of the well were some dried-up vines hanging down, so he grabbed hold of one and lowered himself into the well. When the bandits went right past the well without seeing him, the man thought he was safe. But when he looked down, he saw six poisonous snakes writhing at the bottom, so he decided he should climb out of the well. But then he saw that five large rats at the top of the well were gnawing at the brittle vine. If the rats gnawed through the vine, he would fall into the snake pit. So, he thought he'd better climb out quickly, but as he started climbing he heard the bandits coming back. What to do? He could neither climb out of the well nor go back down.

The Buddha likened this man's situation to sentient beings who are not yet enlightened. The four bandits symbolize the four elements of earth, air, fire, and water. The five rats are the five skandhas, and the snakes are the six realms of existence. Every possible way out was a threat that was pressing in. And that is like the situation for all of us, being pressed in by phenomena—the four elements, the five skandhas, and in the six realms of existence. In this story the only way out for the man is to disappear. Then, the four elements, the five skandhas, and the six realms of existence cannot harm him. The vanishing of that man is a metaphor for the realization of emptiness. If a person can realize emptiness, at that moment, he is free from all phenomenal threats. This story illustrates the idea that it sometimes takes a close brush with death to realize the need to practice with diligence.

BUDDHA IS
MEDICINE FOR
SENTIENT BEINGS

Commentary on a Letter from
Chan Master Dahui Zonggao

Buddha is medicine for sentient beings. If sentient beings'
illness is alleviated, then there's no longer a need for the
medicine. Yet, there is a case where the disease is alleviated
but the medicine is still kept around. This is when one can
enter the realm of the buddhas but cannot enter the realm
of Mara. This disease goes hand in hand with all those
other diseases that sentient beings have not yet gotten rid
of. When the disease and the medicine are both gotten rid
of and both the buddhas and Mara are swept away, then
you will begin to be only in partial accordance with this
great matter of causes and conditions.

If you desire to empty the myriad things, then, you must
first purify your own mind. When your own mind is puri-
fied, the various conditions will cease. Once conditions
cease, the essence and function of your mind become thus:
The essence is the fundamental origin of your pure mind.
The function is the wondrous workings of your transformative mind. At that time, you will not be stained when

you enter the realm of purity or defilement. If you reach this field likened to the windless ocean and the cloudless sky, then you can be called "one who learns from the Buddha." If you have not yet attained this state, you should hastily bring forth your zeal.

—from a letter by MASTER DAHUI TO A DISCIPLE

Affirming the Self

The purpose of practice is to ultimately let go of the sense of self, but in the beginning we need to affirm the self as the vehicle for practice. This is what we are doing when we begin meditating by relaxing our body and mind. Then we settle the mind by contemplating the breath going in and out of the nostrils. As we do these things, we are aware of who is relaxing, who is breathing. The idea is to reflect this awareness back to ourselves as the one who is experiencing them—we collect these scattered thoughts back to a focal point in our mind.

To affirm your sense of self, use the awareness of your whole being as a point of reference, so that your pain, drowsiness, and wandering thoughts bring you back to your own reality. There is no need to go any further than drawing your scattered mind back to this moment. Once the mind is concentrated, you can begin real huatou practice. After your mind is no longer swayed by the environment, then with a strong sense of self you have a foundation for taking up "What is *wu*?" So, you establish concentration through strengthening this sense of self. At that point, you start using "What is *wu*?" as a point of entry to practice. But, without establishing a strong, focused sense of self, your practice will have no foundation, as if you were floating.

Conceptually, *wu* means "empty," "no," or "not." How does this relate to the sense of self? You play several roles in life that can change from one moment to another. Which one is really you? It must be *wu*, no-self, because there is no fixed, abiding, and unchanging "you" in any of the roles you play. In each instant, you are constantly changing and breathing. Who is changing and breathing? You're experiencing pain. Who is in pain? Normally it is very difficult to focus on asking "What is *wu*?" because your mind is being pulled by wandering thoughts, pain, drowsiness, and so on. You're being pushed and pulled by all these conditions. So, you clarify your chaotic mind by identifying what is happening to yourself. You never have to leave yourself to do this; you just bring these experiences back to the reality of your being there. Once your body is relaxed and your mind is focused, ask yourself, "Who is experiencing this?" Recognize that your "I" plays numerous roles and is constantly in flux. That is *wu;* that is no-self. But what is no-self, then? With this desire to experientially know emptiness, you steer this mind to asking "What is *wu*?" When your mind and body are thus unified, your sole task is to focus on "What is *wu*?" *Wu* becomes your vehicle to awakening, to enlightenment.

To Manifest Wisdom

If in our practice we can always maintain a pure mind, a pure body, and pure speech, we will surely cut off our vexations and make progress toward liberation. In daily life, even though we know the difference between pure and impure, there are times we cannot control ourselves and we act impurely. Therefore to maintain pure mind, body, and speech, we practice meditation. Through meditation we can sense immediately whether our mind is calm or confused. In basic Buddhism the point of meditation is to free the mind of wandering thoughts so that it can enter samadhi. However, in Chan there is this saying: "Do not be concerned with wandering thoughts arising, be concerned with not being aware of them." Chan believes that if there were no wandering thoughts, then there would be no way for wisdom to manifest. In other words, when we are aware of wandering thoughts, it is possible to derive wisdom in that moment. Chan does not consider samadhi in itself to be liberation because after emerging from samadhi, we still have vexations. Rather, Chan emphasizes cultivating wisdom in daily life. Chan wisdom is not some kind of intelligence or special knowledge. It is a state of mind that does not give rise to vexation in the midst of activities. The mind still moves but remains pure. That is the Chan wisdom that expresses the teaching of the Mahayana in its completeness.

Once, my Dharma master Lingyuan asked his grand master Xuyun whether during samadhi thoughts arise in the mind. Xuyun replied that if thoughts arise, one is not in samadhi, but if there were no thought in samadhi, one would be like a wooden statue. Xuyun is saying that no matter how deep the samadhi, there is still attachment. Ordinarily, people can sense only the very coarse or obvious trains of thoughts rising in their mind. A person in samadhi would definitely not give rise to this type of coarse wandering thoughts, but very subtle self-attachment still exists, and this is not true wisdom.

According to the Linji line of Chan, the purpose of investigating huatou is not to experience samadhi by eliminating wandering thoughts, but to manifest wisdom. Indeed, the method itself is a wandering thought, because one keeps asking "What is *wu*?" It may seem paradoxical to ask a huatou for an answer to *wu*, emptiness. In fact, there is no answer. The point is to transform your mind, to collect all your wandering thoughts into just one wandering thought—the huatou. At the point where you can continuously ask the huatou, you will be gradually generating the doubt mass. This doubt mass is actually another wandering thought; not only is it a wandering thought, it also is a vexation because you will have this strong desire for an answer. That seeking an answer is vexation, but this is not ordinary vexation; it is actually another form of the right view.

Let me repeat how you enter the practice of huatou. First, relax your body and mind. Second, when sitting, eating, walking, working, listening, being vexed, being drowsy, be aware of who is experiencing this. With this awareness, you will establish an intimate connection with the self. Keep asking, "Who is experiencing this?" If you enter samadhi, ask yourself, "Who is in samadhi?" Ask this, because even in samadhi there is attachment, and the "you" is not your true self. People can enter samadhi without the help of a master, but at this stage they still need to ask, "Who is in samadhi?"

Do the same for all activities. If you are sweeping the floor, ask, "Who is sweeping the floor?" Of course, with this question in your mind you will not be able to enter samadhi. Actually, the question is itself a wandering thought, but I recommend it because it helps establish the sense of self. As a huatou, however, "Who am I?" cannot generate enough power to get you enlightened. Most likely you will eventually get bored. Therefore, when your mind is settled and you are ready to practice huatou, I recommend "What is *wu*?"

Wu is the state of no-self without vexations. In this state it is possible for true wisdom to arise. Conceptually we all understand *wu*, but unfortunately we are still attached to self-existence. In this practice, if we keep asking "What is *wu*?" eventually, because we really want to understand *wu*, we discover the true wisdom behind this selflessness. So, on the Mahayana path the focus is not on avoiding wandering thoughts but on transforming them into wisdom. If you can find vexation in wandering thoughts, you can also find bodhi-mind itself. You will learn that vexation is wisdom and wisdom is vexation. So, can we all say, "Great! Since I have lots of vexation, then I must have lots of wisdom." No, what I am really saying is that we should use our vexation to open up our wisdom. So, do not get upset with having wandering thoughts and vexations, because if you can locate your wandering thoughts in your vexation, then you actually can find wisdom.

Did any of you use the methods I have talked about? Did you apply them to your practice? Is my advice useful? If not, would you raise your hand?

[*Student raises hand*]

Sheng Yen: Why isn't the method working for you? If you are not getting results, maybe it is because you are looking too hard for enlightenment. This is a common situation. There is pain and discomfort, but like breaking in a new pair of shoes, you have to give it some time. You can't expect to get enlightened after one day.

Student: Since all phenomena are empty, why are we sitting here? Isn't this looking for trouble?

Sheng Yen: You are absolutely correct. Practicing huatou is looking for trouble within yourself. You use it to collect your scattered thoughts into this one question for which you have no answer. The result is that there is no way out for you; you cannot spread it around or look somewhere else, but you still have this urgent desire to know the answer to the huatou.

Student: For the English speakers, why not have them ask "What is emptiness?" instead of "What is *wu?*"

Sheng Yen: Because asking "What is emptiness?" will only give you a conceptual understanding that will also be wrong because you will think that emptiness is just a blank void. That will only make you feel sad.

Student: Since there are many possible huatous, why can't we have personal huatous so we don't all have to practice the same one? Maybe one huatou will speak to one person but not to another.

Sheng Yen: At this store the only thing we sell is *wu.* A pizza store only sells pizza. [*Laughter*]

Student: But there are many selections of pizza at the pizza shop.

Sheng Yen: But it's still pizza. [*Laughter*] OK, thank you. Now let's practice huatou.

Wu and Buddha-Nature

Beginning tonight, I will comment on a text from the record of Chan Master Dahui Zonggao. Dahui was a great advocate of the huatou method and in particular, "What is *wu*?" This huatou can be traced to a story from the Tang dynasty in which Chan Master Zhaozhou was asked by a monk, "Does a dog have buddha-nature?" To this question Master Zhaozhou answered, "*Wu*," which essentially means "No!" The monk was dumbfounded by this answer because Buddhism teaches that all sentient beings, including dogs, have buddha-nature. So what did Master Zhaozhou mean?

Of course, Master Zhaozhou was not ignorant of the teaching that all sentient beings have buddha-nature. However, by answering *wu* to the monk's question, he cut off the questioner's stream of wandering thoughts. If he had answered yes, the next question might have been, "Why are there no dog buddhas?" And more questions would have followed upon that one. All these questions would be irrelevant to the monk's attention to his own practice. To cut off the trivial chatter, Zhaozhou answered no directly.

The record of this encounter between Zhaozhou and the monk is called a *gong'an*, which, as I have explained above, literally means "public case." Relating this gong'an to your own practice, the huatou serves the same function of cutting off deluded thinking by looking into this single word, *wu*. After all, there's nothing behind this nothingness; there's no room for bargaining, no room for a conceptualization. So, in practicing this huatou, "What is *wu*?" the first step is to cut off your train of deluded thoughts. The second step is to generate a doubt sensation on the basis of this huatou, and perhaps you too will reach enlightenment.

This state of *wu* is closely connected with the truth of nonattachment, for if wandering thoughts and attachments are severed, then *wu* will manifest. This state is free from self-centeredness because deluded thinking and attachments *are* the self. This state is no-self, also known in Chan as no-form and no-thought.

Dahui's text is taken from a letter to one of his lay disciples:

Buddha is medicine for sentient beings. If sentient beings' illness is alleviated, then there's no longer a need for the medicine. Yet, there is a case where the disease is alleviated but the medicine is still kept around. This is when one can enter the realm of the buddhas but cannot enter the realm of Mara. This disease goes hand in hand with all those other diseases that sentient beings have not yet gotten rid of. When the disease and the medicine are both gotten rid of and both the buddhas and Mara are swept away, then you will begin to be only in partial accordance with this great matter of causes and conditions.

If we take Buddha as a medicine, then if our sickness is cured, we don't need the medicine anymore. But after our sickness is cured, some of us still keep the medicine around. If a practitioner were truly liberated, there would no longer be a need for medicine. If he or she still holds on to the medicine, for that person the sickness has not really been cured. As the text says, it is like a person who can enter the realm of the buddhas but cannot enter the demonic realm of Mara. In Buddhism "Mara" refers to, among other meanings, the Lord of the Dead. The reason this person cannot enter the realm of Mara is because they still see buddhas and maras as separate: There is something pure, the buddhas, and there is something impure, the maras. So, holding on to the medicine after one is cured is another illness, for if the disease is really cured, both buddhas and maras can be swept away. If one can be in accordance with this, then they are said to be in partial accordance with why Shakyamuni Buddha appeared—to liberate sentient beings from both buddhas and maras.

A buddha is someone who is fully enlightened and who, at the same time, can help others become enlightened. Being fully enlightened means being completely cured of vexations and afflictions. Being completely cured, a buddha is also a doctor who can give appropriate medicine to others. So, in "Buddha is medicine for sentient beings," Dahui says that the Buddha's teaching is a cure for the suffering brought upon by our being afflicted by the kleshas, the three poisons of greed, aversion, and ignorance.

For most people, when their body is sick, their mind is also troubled; this gives rise to vexations and afflictions, and this is called suffering. Yet, in principle one's body can experience pain, but the mind need not be afflicted. In themselves our life experiences may not be suffering, but they give rise to emotions that are experienced as suffering. So when the Buddha spoke about the suffering of birth, sickness, old age, and death, he was referring to the endless cycle of birth and death, samsara.

To be specific, sentient beings have three kinds of afflictions: conceptual, emotive, and fundamental. Conceptual afflictions are hindrances or vexations pertaining to your view of things; emotive afflictions pertain to how you feel about your own being, which may be different from your conceptual views; fundamental affliction is the most subtle and is called ignorance, or *avidya* in Sanskrit. When a person first becomes enlightened, that person is said to have attained the correct view about the nature of existence, and therefore will have terminated conceptual afflictions. But one is still far from extinguishing all their emotional afflictions. Only when a person reaches buddhahood will all of the emotional afflictions be terminated. And the third type, fundamental ignorance, can actually be subsumed under the category of emotional afflictions, except that it is the most subtle, most fundamental, deep-rooted of afflictions. And that, of course, is only extinguished when one reaches buddhahood.

This all sounds very technical, and you may wonder, "What

does this have to do with me?" Actually you don't have to remember any of what I just said, but your real practice begins only when you realize you have lots of vexations. And though erroneous views are terminated when you become enlightened, you will still have vexations. However, because you have experienced genuine emptiness, you will also have more confidence and faith. Although your practice may falter at times, your faith and confidence will remain, and you will most likely practice again.

I have already described the three stages to the huatou practice. The first is *reciting*, the second is *asking*, and the third is *investigating*. Actually, there's a fourth stage that occurs after enlightenment. It is called "*watching* the huatou." Why does one need to watch the huatou? Because vexations are still around, you need to keep watching the huatou so you can see how the vexations operate within you and how you can gradually leave them behind.

> If sentient beings' illness is alleviated, then there's no longer
> a need for the medicine.

How do sentient beings alleviate their spiritual illness? In Chan there is the sudden approach and there is the gradual approach. "Sudden" refers to the instantaneous termination of erroneous views, while "gradual" refers to the slow process of wearing away afflictions. In fact, Dahui's statement includes both aspects. When sudden enlightenment happens, the part of our illness that holds erroneous views is alleviated. Hearing this, you may have high hopes, and indeed, somewhere there may be a person who goes on retreat, hears the Dharma, meditates, and lo and behold, becomes enlightened! On the other hand, some may take longer, depending on the depth of their virtuous karmic roots. When the karmic roots are ready, they sprout. So, if a person has deep karmic roots, merely encountering the Dharma can spark that virtuous karma, causing that person to reach enlightenment. But the stock of good karma within sentient beings differs. According to the Buddhist treatise called *The Awakening of Mahayana Faith,* the time it takes to reach the state where one's faith will no longer regress—essentially where they experience enlightenment—is ten thousand kalpas. However, if I were to tell you it will take ten thousand kalpas to experience enlightenment, then probably this Chan Hall would be empty. But you should not belittle yourselves, because the very fact you are here shows that you have a very good share of virtuous karma.

We should not take too literally the idea in *The Awakening of Mahayana Faith* of enlightenment taking ten thousand aeons, since that refers to someone who constantly regresses. Indeed, after seeing their buddha-nature, they will not regress. Relating this to our own practice, we can understand how the treatise would say something like this, because our own faith vacillates. One day we have total confidence in the Dharma, and on other days we backslide. In and out, we sometimes give rise to doubt, sometimes exude confidence. So if one practices very diligently and with utmost effort, then ten thousand kalpas may not seem that long.

Dahui says that if the illness is alleviated, there is no longer a need for medicine. As I mentioned before, this illness can be alleviated suddenly or gradually. When the text says, "illness is alleviated," you can take that to mean completely gone. So, if one is cured, do you think they need any more medicine? No. Similarly, if someone reaches buddhahood, they will keep the medicine around to spread the Buddha's teaching. But would a buddha carry around sutras, saying, "This is a Buddhist sutra; it is very good for you. Take it." [*Laughter*] Definitely not. If one has already attained buddhahood, the words coming out of one's mouth will be sutras. That should be very clear.

My question for you is, do you believe you have virtuous karmic roots? Do you believe it will take you ten thousand kalpas to see your self-nature? Buddhism is a medicine for sentient beings; when illness is alleviated, there is no longer a need for medicine. For you to come here during your Christmas break is evidence of having good karmic roots, and you don't have to think of yourself as starting from the first kalpa. For all you know, you may have completed 9,999 kalpas already. [*Laughter*] One kalpa can go by very quickly; it depends on your diligence.

Buddhas and Maras

Tonight we continue with Dahui's letter to a disciple:

> Yet, there is a case where the disease is alleviated but the medicine is still kept around. This is when one can enter the realm of the buddhas but cannot enter the realm of Mara.

The dualistic mind is the mind of discrimination, clinging to the idea of buddhas as good and pure as opposed to Mara, who is bad and impure. So, when one thinks they are free from Dharma illness yet clings to the idea of being in the realm of the buddhas, the sickness has not really been alleviated. A person who has a headache takes a pill, but when the headache is gone, what should he do with the rest of the bottle? He puts it back in the medicine cabinet, because the potential for another headache is still there. When he sees other people with headaches, he will have compassion and say, "Here, take this tablet." When I was in Rome visiting the ambassador, I had a headache and the ambassador's wife gave me some headache tablets. I said, "Do you always carry these to help people with headaches?" She said, "It's because I myself often have headaches." So this is like a compassionate bodhisattva who would share the Dharma-medicine with others.

An aspiring bodhisattva can be alleviated from vexations, and it may seem like they are already liberated, but the potential for future vexations is still present. Therefore, they still need Dharma; they still need buddhas; and there are still sentient beings to be helped. At the final stage of liberation where illness is completely gone, a bodhisattva will not have ideas of buddhas and maras. To this bodhisattva, the Lord Buddha and the Lord Mara are just sentient beings. When Shakyamuni attained full enlightenment, he proclaimed that sentient beings are endowed with the meritorious virtue and complete wisdom of the *tathagatas,* or "buddhas." This means that even the demon Mara is endowed with buddha-nature. A fully liberated person can freely enter the realm of the buddhas or the realm of Mara. However, if a practitioner who is not yet liberated takes Buddha and Mara as the same, that person becomes a disciple of Mara and holds erroneous views.

When Dahui says, "One can enter the realm of the buddhas but cannot enter the realm of Mara," he means that one who can enter the realm of the buddhas should also be able to enter the realm of Mara. Conversely, if someone cannot enter the realm of the buddhas, they cannot enter the realm of Mara since they are already there—a prisoner has no choice but to live in prison. Similarly, an unenlightened person has no choice but to live in the realm of delusion. On the other hand, to one who has entered the realm of the buddhas, Buddha and Mara are the same. Having no idea of self and without dualistic views, a liberated sentient being can roam within the realms of buddhas or demons at will. To such a person, maras may simply be acting the role of an evil one. For all we know, this could be a great bodhisattva assuming the guise of a mara to help sentient beings.

When the disease and the medicine are both gotten rid of and both the buddhas and Mara are swept away, then you will begin to be only in partial accordance with this great matter of causes and conditions.

When you are fully liberated, there is no longer need for medicine, and you certainly have freed yourself from this illness. At that time notions of buddhas and maras simply do not exist. Do not take this literally to mean you should take a broom and sweep buddhas and maras away. If you have even the slightest intention of doing that, you still have a dualistic view that there is something to get rid of. So, "both the buddhas and Mara are swept away" simply means that in your mind there is no attachment to either Buddha or Mara. However, being a Chan practitioner using the huatou method, you should directly take the attitude of a buddha to deal with your afflictions. This is the real meaning of the sudden practice—you directly deal with your afflictions. So, emulating the Buddha, whatever discriminating thoughts arise in your mind, take up the jeweled sword and cut through them. What is this jeweled sword? In fact, you have it already. This jeweled sword is none other than your huatou. Whatever attachment arises, use the sword to cut it down. Then, this sword will become a vajra sword, the diamond sword used by a vajra king.

The right way to practice huatou is to use it like a vajra sword and slash away anything that confronts you. Wandering thoughts—cut them away. Drowsiness—cut it down. If ten thousand answers to your huatou appear, use the huatou to cut them down and just continue with the asking. Otherwise, you will easily give in and lose the battle. The swordlike huatou you are using is miraculous. It has no enemies, because any enemy who appears will be slashed down. If ten thousand enemies appear, merely showing your sword will repel them. That is the strength of your sword, and you should have confidence in that.

At a gathering of the Buddha's disciples, as the Buddha approached, everyone was happy and greeted him with praises, eager to hear him give a sermon. Except for Manjushri Bodhisattva, who drew his sword and chased the Buddha away. You might think, "How dare Manjushri act in such a rude way to the Buddha?" However, someone who understands the meaning of the sword will see that Manjushri's intention was not to offend the Buddha, but to show the others that a liberated person uses the vajra sword to cut away even attachment to the idea of Buddha.

There's a saying among some Chinese Buddhists that in moments of dire need, one should hold on dearly to the Buddha's foot. But this kind of reliance on something outside oneself is spiritually immature. So, tomorrow night when I come in here, I'll see which one of you will take up the incense board and chase me away. But you won't fool me, because I'll be able to tell whether you're just pretending or really demonstrating some understanding. [*Laughter*]

In the course of practice, you will meet two kinds of enemies. The first you already know about because you face them all the time—wandering thoughts and pain. Again, continue to use your huatou to overcome these enemies, but be aware of another kind of enemy. Typically, they are very beautiful or pleasurable. For example, a sitting where you experience complete peace; your mind is tranquil and focused, and you feel that you've lost the burden of your body. In the midst of that you give rise to a thought: "This is truly pleasurable." So, you expect the next period to be the same and the period after that. And sure enough, you have entered the realm of Mara. You should take up the sword and slash the thought to pieces. Do not anticipate pleasurable states, just as you would not attach to negative experiences. Both are your enemies. If there is the slightest bit of attachment, you have fallen into the trap of Mara.

After they experience such bliss, some people will try to recapture it, but that is simply an attachment. Even if you came up with a formula to regain that state, you are still attached to the pleasure and have not overcome your enemy. The pleasurable and the unpleasant states are equal to one another; attachments to both should be gotten rid of.

When your practice is not going well and you are obstructed, that too is a time to rely on your huatou. Remember to maintain a relaxed body and mind, for then you have a chance to let go of both.

If you cannot even relax body and mind, you will cause yourself more trouble down the road. So, use your huatou steadily without interruption, and make sure your body and mind are relaxed. So this is the meaning of "sweeping away buddhas and Mara."

Some of you are hesitant and have doubts about the huatou. This very indecisiveness is causing you trouble. Since you are here already, do not worry about the future. Take up the huatou, and just simply and directly use it. Relax, and allow no interruption to your questioning. Use the huatou and slash away attachments to both pleasure and discomfort. If you practice accordingly, then you will accord with the meaning of Dahui's teaching.

To Empty the Myriad Things

We will continue with our commentary on the text by Dahui Zonggao:

> If you desire to empty the myriad things, then, you must first purify your own mind. When your own mind is purified, the various conditions will cease. Once conditions cease, the essence and function of your mind become thus: The essence is the fundamental origin of your pure mind. The function is the wondrous workings of your transformative mind. At that time, you will not be stained when you enter the realm of purity or defilement. If you reach this field likened to the windless ocean and the cloudless sky, then you can be called "one who learns from the Buddha." If you have not yet attained this state, you should hastily bring forth your zeal.

If you want to "empty the myriad things," meaning our vexations and suffering, you must first purify your mind. Once the mind is pure, the myriad negative conditions naturally cease. At that time, true suchness is revealed as the essence of mind, and the karma-free acts of body, speech, and mind are its functions. Your original nature as true suchness will manifest as pure mind, and you will not discriminate between purity and defilement. Therefore, you can enter both the pure realm and the defiled realm and not be stained. Dahui likens a mind free of afflictions to an utterly calm sea, while the mind's infinite spaciousness is like a cloudless sky.

Emptying your mind does not mean destroying everything in it; rather, it means detaching the mind from all its afflictions and attachments. If you can do this, then you are "one who learns from the Buddha." If you relate this idea to your life, you will see that it is extremely difficult to do. Perhaps the most concrete example is the fear of dying, which ultimately means losing your sense of self.

Sometimes the very people who have the strongest cravings say, "Me? I don't have any craving." However, sometimes it is just because they have not had the opportunity to give in to desire.

This advice to purify your mind is directed at practitioners with the sharpest karmic roots, because ordinary people find it easier to purify their conduct than their mind. Without pure conduct, how can your mind be pure? So, if you can at least uphold the precepts, you will condition your mind to also be pure. There's a Chinese saying, "One should guard their body as if it were a precious jade." So, by upholding precepts, your mind will gradually be transformed. If you say, "Mind is more important, so I should purify my mind first," this is a grave mistake for beginners. How can you have a pure mind and your conduct be sloppy and improper?

Pure mind is not something that we acquire, that we gain after some time of practice. In fact, pure mind has always been there as part of our fundamental nature. But, along with this pure mind there are also vexations and fundamental ignorance. The purpose of practice is to allow this pure mind of true suchness to reveal itself. Practice is thus likened to regaining the luminosity of this pure mind, allowing it to shine forth. But even though pure mind is inherent, since it is obstructed by fundamental ignorance, delusion, and vexation, we must practice. So, the purpose of a method is not really to acquire some presumably better state, but to shake off vexations and ignorance. Once the shell of ignorance and vexation is shaken off, then true suchness naturally manifests. Imagine a dog outside in the snow: The snow covers the dog to the point where we can't tell that it's a dog. It's just a snow animal. Then it goes under a tree, shakes, and the snow falls off, and the dog underneath is revealed.

This is like using the huatou method. You investigate it until you build up this great mass of doubt. When that doubt shatters, then, at least temporarily, vexation, ignorance, and delusion depart, leaving you with the pure mind of your original nature. So, seeing the dog shaking off the snow is likened to seeing your self-nature. But if the dog goes back out, the snow can collect again, so it has to again and again shake off the snow. It is an unending process, until even the dog disappears. Even if it's still snowing, there is no dog for the snow to fall on, and that is like the pure mind of complete enlightenment.

In Chan, another term for this pure mind is "no-mind," meaning there is no mind to be conditioned by vexations; there is no mind that can be influenced by the external environment. Thus no-mind means the same thing as no-self, and no-self is also complete enlightenment.

"Various conditions" refers to opportunities for vexations and delusions to arise—all the negativities. So, when you reach a state of no-mind (no-self), on the one hand there is no self-clinging to negativity, and on the other hand vexations have no place to settle; on the one hand the practitioner stays out of trouble; on the other hand trouble can't find the practitioner—vexations and afflictions simply do not arise.

The treatise *The Awakening of Mahayana Faith* says, "When the mind arises, the manifold dharmas [phenomena] also arise; when the mind ceases, the myriad dharmas also cease to be." "Mind" here refers to the mind of vexations. So, when vexations are born out of true suchness, you can be sure that whatever confronts you is vexation. Similarly, when vexations are divorced from the mind of true suchness (these two coexist), then phenomena and situations will no longer be vexatious. This statement clearly describes the relationship between pure mind, the mind of vexations, and the myriad things.

Here is something we should reflect on: This person was on his deathbed with cancer and in excruciating pain. His mind was full of vexations, fear, resentment, and resistance—the myriad things. But then he used the method of contemplating emptiness, and as the myriad things began to cease, he saw emptiness in the pain, and that the body was empty as well. This is one example of emptying the mind of myriad conditions. This man's story shows that when the mind contemplates emptiness, vexations and even external events can change for the better.

Prior to realizing pure mind, what should you do? Use your huatou like a vajra sword and cut away attachments. Whatever wandering or deluded thoughts, whatever attachments arise, cut them down. Be like a volcano with hot lava bubbling inside, and wandering thoughts and vexations are snowflakes falling from the sky. When the snowflakes fall into the volcano, they simply melt away. That is the power of the huatou—to melt away vexations. Believe in the power of your huatou. As soon as you have vexations, bring forth this huatou and ask the question. Your vexations will melt like snowflakes falling in hot lava.

So, if tonight a ghost or spirit appears before you, what should you do? Just ask, "What is *wu*?" And I will bet he can't answer, or he will say, "I don't know *wu*," and vanish.

Student: He'll get enlightened. [*Laughter*]

Sheng Yen: That's good. Before you get enlightened yourself, you help a ghost get enlightened. [*Laughter*] That's very good. You will have delivered at least one sentient being. [*Laughter*] Then the enlightened ghost will turn around and start teaching you: "Look at you! You're not enlightened. You're the one who's a ghost!" We will stop here. Don't forget to use your huatou like that live volcano. It should be a live volcano, not a dead one.

True Suchness

Let us continue our commentary on Dahui's text:

> Once conditions cease, the essence and function of your mind become thus: The essence is the fundamental origin of your pure mind. The function is the wondrous workings of your transformative mind. At that time, you will not be stained when you enter the realm of purity or defilement. If you reach this field likened to the windless ocean and the cloudless sky, then you can be called "one who learns from the Buddha." If you have not yet attained this state, you should hastily bring forth your zeal.

"Conditions" here refers to whatever is in the field of our five senses as well as the mind faculty, which we can call the "sixth sense." In the spatial dimension, conditions are whatever corresponds to the five senses, whatever is seen, heard, touched, smelled, tasted. In the temporal dimension they are all of the symbols, language, words, ideas that we create in our mind. All of these things exist in our memory, and they also exist because of our projection into the future—in other words, everything that is in our thought-stream. In fact, this mental continuum is simply a conglomeration of symbols: words, language, all relative to each other as well as to the sense of self. So, spatially we have the sense objects of the five sense organs, or faculties, and temporally we have the objects of the sixth sense faculty, which is mind.

[*Claps his hands*] Is this a condition to you? Conditioned

mind has two aspects: on the one hand it is constantly clinging to the five sense objects plus the mind's activities; on the other hand the same sense objects are being conditioned by external phenomena. When we practiced contemplation of emptiness and direct contemplation, I asked you not to allow your mind to be caught up by what you were experiencing. I asked you not to allow the objects of your meditation take over the content of your mind. Do not label, describe, or compare what you are seeing or hearing. If you do any of these things, then it is a conditioned mind. Again, on the one hand the mind is clinging to these forms or sounds; on the other hand these forms and sounds are conditioning the mind. They have taken over the mind's content, and on the basis of that, the mind generates more conceptual ideas and deluded thinking. So, if I clap my hands, that itself may not necessarily condition your mind, but it is conditioning if you conceive of me clapping my hands, giving it a label.

On the basis of that you generate more thoughts: "Why is Shifu clapping his hands?" But if you hear and perceive the sound just as a pure phenomenon, without adding to or wanting something from it, your mind is not being conditioned. So, originally your mind flowed freely and was free from conditions; but because of your habit of clinging, you get stuck on experience. The mind encounters something and gets stuck on it, and generates more thoughts and elaborations. But in the state of no-mind, of total nonattachment, the mind perceives everything without getting caught up in clinging. As soon as you generate some kind of clinging, then no-mind transforms into conditioned mind.

One thing I should say is that sentient beings cannot help but live in a conditioned way. That is because the basic factor that conditions the mind, self-grasping, still exists. So, when the text says "once conditions cease," that is, when this grasping ceases, then one's mind will no longer be conditioned.

A few words are needed to explain the meaning of "essence"

and "function." We can understand essence to be the true mind, the original, unconditioned mind. There are many words for this in Buddhism: unconditioned mind, true mind, pure mind, true suchness. Once free from self-grasping, the wondrous mind naturally returns to its original state and manifests two kinds of wisdom: The first is *fundamental wisdom* that severs afflictions; when this type of wisdom manifests, afflictions are absent. A second type of wisdom is *acquired wisdom,* which responds to the external world. Since one is free from self-grasping and attachment, the only response possible for someone with acquired wisdom is compassionate deliverance of sentient beings. One relates to others on the basis of what they need. With these two types of wisdom, a person is said to abide in suchness, a state characterized by three qualities: being natural without pretense, being at ease, and being free from any restraint or bondage.

The essence is the fundamental origin of your pure mind.

From the perspective of pure mind, there is no such thing as defiled mind. Pure mind is simply the fundamental, original state of being that has always been there. Furthermore, it is not something that is gained after some time of practice—it has been there all the time; it is just that fundamental ignorance and affliction have also been there. Therefore, the point of practice is not to acquire this pure mind or to gain enlightenment; it is rather more like restoring the mind's original state of purity. How do we do that? We just get rid of all those things that are obscuring the purity. And what are those things? They are none other than our vexations and attachments. So, once these things are gotten rid of, the mind realizes its natural state of purity. So, even though Dahui speaks of the origin of pure mind, it is only in conventional terms. From the perspective of true suchness, pure mind is without an origin.

The function is the wondrous workings of your transformative mind.

"Function" refers to true suchness as manifested in the complete enlightenment of great bodhisattvas and buddhas. When the mind regains this original state of being, it is free, unhindered, and able to help sentient beings. However, just saying that one is able to help sentient beings is limiting because, at that time, this function of the mind is limitless. First of all we should not think of it as just a one-to-one relationship with sentient beings. Rather, the mind of true suchness can respond to many sentient beings at the same time and in many places; this is not ordinary enlightenment but that of the highest buddhas and bodhisattvas. So, it is not the case that the mind of true suchness is static and inert; indeed one is even more responsive because of "the wondrous workings of your transformative mind."

The Chinese name for Avalokiteshvara Bodhisattva is Guanyin, which can be translated as "Contemplation of Freedom." This freedom can be understood as freedom of body and freedom of mind, and only the highest bodhisattvas achieve this. "Freedom of body" means that the great bodhisattvas can manifest in different realms of existence at the same time, helping numerous sentient beings simultaneously. In terms of the stages of the bodhisattva path, this unlimited freedom is only attained in the stage prior to buddhahood.

At that time, you will not be stained even when you enter the realm of defilement [in order to deliver sentient beings].

How shall we understand this? When a person has fully realized the pure mind of true suchness, then that individual will no longer cling to conditions. You can liken this to having immunity to any kind of mental affliction. Because of this, they can freely enter anywhere. When they enter the samsaric world of suffering, they will not be conditioned by it. Incarnated buddhas can get sick like any sentient being, but their mind will not be affected. Similarly, they can freely roam in the buddha realms or in different world systems. In either case the mind is free and at ease.

Dahui compares this pure mind to a windless ocean and cloudless sky. This is the idea of the unconditioned mind not clinging to anything, like the ocean without any wind and therefore no waves, completely serene. In a cloudless sky nothing obstructs the luminosity; so not only is this mind stable and peaceful, it is utterly clear and bright. Master Dahui's ocean is a metaphor for no-mind, but we should not push this analogy too far, because ocean and clouds are still phenomena, whereas no-mind is completely free of forms or obstructions.

> If you reach this field likened to the windless ocean and the cloudless sky, then you can be called "one who learns from the Buddha."

Actually, this does not mean Master Dahui is setting an impossibly high standard. Rather, Dahui is talking about one who has fulfilled the task of realizing pure mind as "one who learns from the Buddha." At the very least, we have learned from the Buddha if we have actually experienced that our self-nature is empty. Such a person would at least have an inkling of unobstructed mind. Everything we have said to this point refers to the enlightened state. What about those of us who are not enlightened? Well, we should just continue to work diligently on our huatou.

Why should we understand this "lofty" state of enlightenment when we are not nearly there yet? Well, have you heard that the best chocolate is made in Switzerland? So, talking about enlightenment is a bit like talking about Swiss chocolate to someone who has never tasted it. The hearer may even drool. One time when I was going to Italy, someone said, "If you go there, you have to have their ice cream. It is the best." So, in Italy we went for some ice cream. I myself cannot eat ice cream because it is too cold for my stomach, so I watched my disciples and other people eat. I asked them, "How is it?" They all said, "Very good." And all I could do was watch and drool. [*Laughter*] So, that's what I'm doing here: talking about enlightenment to lure all of you. All the talks and discourse records of the Chan masters are really meant to encourage practitioners who are not yet enlightened. But hearing about oceans without waves and cloudless skies might urge people to strive for awakening. [*Laughter*]

Stages on the Path of Enlightenment

Chan has no stages. But for the purpose of discussion, we can describe the Chan path to enlightenment as consisting of passing through four stages. However, when we speak of stages, we are not talking about something absolute or even saying that one has to traverse all the levels. Everyone's experience is unique, but there are four more or less distinct levels of experience in the path to Chan enlightenment. The first three levels can easily be mistaken for genuine or true enlightenment, but according to Chan, they are not.

The first stage arises out of samadhi and is experienced as bliss—often as limitless expanses of light and beautiful sound. Because this experience can be so powerful, one feels that they have been liberated. However, when one comes out of samadhi and returns to daily life, they are again subject to vexations. While it is good, this experience is not enlightenment.

A second stage is the feeling of extreme peace and purity, as if one had transcended time and space. This state arises out of an even deeper samadhi than the first level, and one can also easily mistake it for enlightenment. The difference is that coming out of this state, one can remain free of vexations for a long time. Like the first level, while it is a good stage to experience, it is still not enlightenment, because there is still attachment to the experience.

Because of their attachment to the idea of enlightenment, people grasp at these experiences, which are actually manifestations of their good karmic roots, and they misinterpret them. In the worst cases, people are so eager for experiences that they become prey to external spirits who use them as a vehicle for their own agendas. All of this is due to a lack of correct views and the proper guidance of a teacher. Therefore, in Dharma practice, what is primary is correct view, and ultimately the correct view is the view of the nature of emptiness.

The third stage is actually the first level of experience where one genuinely experiences a glimpse of emptiness. A person at this stage does not view the world in the same way an ordinary person does. One has experienced awakening, but if there is a thought of having achieved enlightenment, then they are dwelling in this experience of emptiness and that is also an attachment. One can call this "seeing one's buddha-nature," and it can be considered shallow enlightenment, but it is not the ultimate enlightenment.

To go beyond emptiness and attain true enlightenment, one needs to dissolve the attachment to emptiness itself. When that happens, one feels that all things manifest and exist without any obstruction whatsoever. So, one must go beyond emptiness itself in order to realize the great awakening. However, having arrived at this stage, one must still practice in order not to regress. This fourth stage is what I would confirm as true enlightenment.

I have two phrases that may give you an idea of the experience of great awakening. The first is, "The whole world has collapsed and is sunken." Material existence has vanished, and please don't ask where it has sunken to. The second phrase is, "Empty space is shattered." Enlightenment is something like that—everything that is tangible collapses and vanishes. Anything you can use to identify your sense of self is gone. It would be a mistake to view enlighten-ment as transcending the material world, but you experience both the substantial and the nonsubstantial being shattered. That leaves you with nothing to identify with, nothing to cling to, no place to stand on. This experience of emptiness is ineffable, but these phrases give you an idea.

However, if you come to interview and say, "Shifu, I have expe-rienced the collapse of the world and the shattering of empty space," that would be unacceptable. Obviously, the ground you stand on is still there, the space around you is still there; everything is still there.

This is really what Dahui means when he says "various condi-tions will cease." But when everything ceases, what is left? "What can I rely on? Where can I gain a footing?" Well, if you still enter-tain thoughts like this, you will not be enlightened. If you think that enlightenment means you will be some kind of lonely spirit floating around with nothing to rely on, you will definitely not be enlightened. Why? Because it is precisely this clinging to self that prevents enlightenment. So, when you are totally free of self-grasp-ing, that is enlightenment. Once grasping, clinging, conditioning, and ultimately, any reliance on things are gotten rid of, at that very moment you are enlightened.

All this may make you feel that enlightenment is too remote, too difficult. Instead, you think you should follow the gradual path of cultivating samadhi, but the gradual path is also difficult. However, there is something you *can* do: if in daily life you can let go of all self-grasping and clinging, at that moment you may experi-ence a taste of emptiness. This is the samadhi of the Mahayana way, a direct way to enlightenment. How should you do this in daily life? The answer is to always bring forth your huatou: when you have a chance, pick up and ask the huatou; use it to gain the correct views of impermanence, conditioned arising, and, with that, emptiness.

Here is what else you can do: when beset with afflictions,

contemplate emptiness. How do you do this? Basically, tell yourself that everything is impermanent and without lasting self-identity. If this helps to reduce your vexations, this is fine. Even though you have not really experienced true emptiness, deceiving yourself is sometimes helpful. [*Laughter*] Tell yourself, "Everything I am experiencing is empty." This will help you to give up vexations and, at the same time, become more familiar with emptiness and impermanence. That is very good practice. So, the best time to contemplate emptiness is when you have vexations. This simple and direct method is like those popular books for "idiots." This one is called *Chan Practice for Idiots*. [*Laughter*]

However, please do not misuse the teaching of emptiness. You cannot go home and tell your wife that she is empty. [*Laughter*] And about the responsibilities on your shoulders, you can't escape them by saying, "You're empty too." [*Laughter*] That would be wrong. I have concluded my talks for this retreat, but I have one last piece of advice: if you want to practice the gradual path of samadhi, that's fine, but you are also welcome to directly enter enlightenment by practicing huatou.

THE GREAT MATTER
OF BIRTH
AND DEATH

Commentary on an Excerpt from
the Discourse Record of Dahui Zonggao

Whether drinking tea or eating your meal, always fix at the tip of your nostrils the two affairs of not knowing where you were born and where you will go after death. Amidst quiet places or noisy places, thought after thought, it should be as if you owed ten thousand or hundreds of dollars without any means of paying the debt. Feeling anxious and suffocated without exits behind, you cannot live and you cannot die. At this time [attachment to] past good and evil can be severed. When you experience this, you can gain power.

Have you not heard the words of the ancient worthy ones that all the Dharma spoken by the Buddha is for the purpose of delivering all kinds of minds? If there's no mind, of what use is all the Dharma?

Most of the literati who study this path seek after quick results. Before the master even opens his mouth to speak, these people will have already formulated a conceptual understanding with their minds, thoughts, and perceptions. When obstructions creep up on them, they lose all control; they become busy with their hands and feet without having anything to hold on to. They don't know that it is actually their conceptual understanding that will take them to King Yama to receive the blows of the iron rod and swallow the blazing iron ball. The person who seeks after quick results is none other than you. And so it is said that those who wish to acquire it will lose it. Those who try to be meticulous will end up being more negligent. The tathagata considers such people pitiable.

In recent times many literati desire to study this path, yet their hearts are not pure; their sickness comes from the fact that poison has entered their hearts. When poison enters the heart, you'll be caught up with whatever you encounter. Being caught up with whatever you encounter, your attachment to the view of the self will grow. As the view of the self increases, all you see and hear will be the shortcomings of other people and you will not be able to take the backward step and briefly examine yourself. "Day by day, after leaving my bed in the morning, what benefit have I brought to myself or others?" One who is able to self-examine like this is called a wise person.

Master Zhaozhou once said, "As for this old monk, besides the two mealtimes of the day when he uses his mind in a complex manner, there are no other occasions where it requires his mind to be complicated." You may wonder where this old fellow is at. If you can recognize his original face, then you can say such things like, "Walking is Chan; sitting is Chan; whether talking, silent, active, or still, everything is at peace." If you are unable to be like this, then you better at all times take the backward step and carefully examine that which is under your own feet. Is it really possible to really know another person's strengths or weaknesses, or to judge whether he or she is an ordinary person or a saint, whether things are truly existent or empty? Pushing and exhausting this self-investigation from one situation to the next until there's nowhere you can drive this questioning, like a mouse getting stuck on the horn of a bull, suddenly you must sever this cunning mind. This is a state where all things will solidify, a place where you can return home and finally firmly sit in peace.

—from the DISCOURSE RECORD OF
MASTER DAHUI ZONGGAO

The Great Matter of Birth and Death

Sometimes, when we are gazing at the moon, clouds will drift by and for a while we have only a hazy view of the moon. But whether we see it clearly or hazily, we know the moon is still there. Practice is something like this—our mind at times becomes hazy, but if we are attentive, we still have a glimpse of the method; we just need to keep it in view when the mind gets cloudy.

Master Dahui Zonggao told us to keep our huatou intact in the four circumstances of walking, standing, sitting, and reclining. Do not allow yourself to be separated from your huatou even when receiving people and dealing with affairs. Take your huatou even to the bathroom. Even if you are diligent, there may be times when wandering thoughts will cause you to lose the huatou, thus giving rise to more wandering thoughts. As you become aware of this, do not punish yourself. Just return to the huatou. The real danger is not being aware of wandering thoughts until it is too late; do not let them take over to the extent there is nothing in your mind but wandering thoughts.

Although you recognize that wandering thoughts will occur, just lock your mind inside the huatou and throw away the key. Your sole concern should be the huatou. If you are constantly shooing flies while eating watermelon, you won't enjoy the watermelon. Likewise, when wandering thoughts fly in and out of your mind, just ignore them and continue with the huatou.

I would like now to begin on my commentary on a discourse by Chan Master Dahui Zonggao:

> Whether drinking tea or eating your meal, always fix at the tip of your nostrils the two affairs of not knowing where you were born and where you will go after death. Amidst quiet places or noisy places, thought after thought, it should be as if you owed ten thousand or hundreds of dollars without any means of paying the debt. Feeling anxious and suffocated without exits behind, you cannot live and you cannot die. At this time [attachment to] past good and evil can be severed. When you experience this, you can gain power.

A practitioner's sole concern should be the great matter of birth and death: What is the purpose of coming into being? How does one deal with death? People crave life and try to avoid death; others live out their life without thinking much about what it means. However, for a Chan practitioner it is fundamental to reflect seriously on birth and death. We call this "giving rise to the doubt sensation." This is not the ordinary doubt of suspicion, but a doubt that springs out of a deep concern, a kind of wondering about and desire to resolve the question of birth and death. Conversely, ignoring the question makes it very difficult to give rise to the doubt sensation. Religions resolve the questions of birth and death through revealed teachings. Chan, on the other hand, does not ask you to believe in anything outside of yourself; it gives you an opportunity to resolve this matter through your own efforts.

In the tradition of Master Linji, the way to resolve the issue of birth and death is to practice huatou. We live as if we will be here tomorrow, but we are not even certain we will live past today. For this reason Dahui advised his students to think of each day as the last day in their life. At the end of your life, what have you accomplished? Where will you go after death? Asking these questions gives you the urgency needed to practice well. Huatou practice can help to settle the mind, but on a more important level, it can help to create the conditions for genuine awakening and resolving the issue of birth and death. So Dahui tells us to keep the attitude like one who has many debts without any means for paying them.

Living in turmoil within ourselves and with others prevents us from enjoying lightness and ease. Dahui characterizes this as not being able to live and not being able to die, not being able to advance or retreat. It is precisely when we feel stuck like this that we can benefit from huatou. Whether in the Chan Hall or in daily life, the method allows us to act with a clear and unperturbed mind. Dahui takes for granted that practitioners know how to regulate their body and mind at a level that allows them to practice with urgency in harsh conditions. It is precisely in adverse situations that we can really gain power from the practice. Imagine Dahui telling us, "After you regulate your mind and your body and you make sure everything is fine with your diet, sleeping conditions, and the environment, then you can start to practice." If we could ensure all that before starting to practice, we would never get around to it. So his approach is to directly use the method at all times and in all situations.

Dahui says that to gain power from adversity, we should investigate *wu*. There is no need to speculate, no need to explain, no knowledge to seek, no teachings to understand, no quietism to practice, no need to wait for enlightenment, and no need to wallow in idleness. He advises us to detach from the old habits of reasoning, of concerning ourselves with buddha-nature, of seeking heightened experiences. There will be times when the mind becomes clear and we think we have realized something. That is also wrong. Only by negating such old habits can we truly use the huatou method. Just ask the question in all its simplicity.

"*Wu?*" is not a question that can be answered with philosophy, nor is it a signpost to enlightenment. What is it then? The answer is that a huatou has no meaning. However, it can be used to free oneself from deluded thinking. The huatou itself does not have that ability; rather, it is the process that frees one from delusion.

I have asked you not to be concerned with wandering thoughts; now I also tell you to let go of the myriad things. On the first level, when you become aware of wandering thoughts, just bring forth your huatou. If you keep doing this, eventually the wandering thoughts will settle down and only the method will remain. At the second level, as you make progress, various "good" and "bad" experiences—the myriad things—will arise. When they come up, just bind yourself to the huatou so that you become it and it becomes you. In time the myriad things will also pass.

When sitting, of course you use the huatou; when prostrating or doing walking meditation, you are still using the huatou. Always keep the huatou in front of you, no matter your situation, but always use it in a relaxed way.

The Place Where Buddhas Are Chosen

To truly shine in athletics, one must undergo rigorous and sometimes harsh training; protégés who are not pushed hard by their coaches are not going to excel. The martial artist Jet Li told me that when he was still a boy his coaches were ruthless. He trained all day, not only with his body and hands, but with all kinds of weapons. After a long day of training, he was often bruised and bleeding. He often thought of quitting, but his goal of being a champion kept him going. Eventually he did become a champion, and a movie star as well. So, to excel in one's field, it is often necessary to endure hardship and discipline.

A meditation hall is a different kind of arena. In Chan we say it is a place where buddhas are chosen. I am referring to the calligraphy at the back of this hall that says, "The place where buddhas are chosen." Imagine how much effort and determination are needed to bring forth the buddha within oneself! Compared to becoming a martial arts champion the discipline, determination, and hardship one must endure to become a buddha is so much greater.

After several days, hopefully you have regulated your body and mind to a point where you can meditate with relative ease. But therein is the pitfall: Your diligence in keeping the huatou in front of you is sometimes present, sometimes not. Or you can just casually recite your huatou as if it were a mantra, "*Wu, wu, wu.*" Proceeding like this, one can sit for a hundred years and never gain an entry. Precisely at the point where your diligence is flagging, you must generate urgency. Where should this urgency come from? It should come from the realization that you have not yet resolved the great matter of birth and death: you do not know your original face before you were born, and you do not know where you will go after you die. In fact, this urgency should come from a sense that you could die tonight, this afternoon, or in the next minute. Knowing the imminence of death, you should earnestly be asking your hua-tou. You must let it engulf you, because you know that you arose from emptiness, and when causes and conditions disperse and you die, that also is emptiness.

You may ask, "What do emptiness and *wu* have to do with me?" If you have no interest in your innate buddha-nature, then it will be difficult to generate the doubt sensation, and without that it is very difficult to realize awakening. Therefore, without knowing your origin and your destination, jump wholeheartedly into *wu* to generate the doubt sensation. This doubt is a kind of wondering; it is an unresolved question that sticks to you. It is not suspicion or skepticism or questioning the truth of something. Rather, it is a not knowing that fills your heart with great urgency, and you have an earnest need to resolve it. Even as you are unable to resolve the doubt, it grows. This state of not knowing, yet wanting earnestly to resolve it, is called "the great ball of doubt." When you shatter this great ball of doubt, awakening ensues.

Therefore, to practice huatou means to ask the question with urgency and earnestness, so that you may generate the doubt sensation. Unless you practice with earnestness, your *wu* will simply become entangled with wandering thoughts, and your mind will wallow in delusion. To truly investigate Chan, you must go beyond merely repeating the huatou; you must bring forth urgency and earnestness.

Having said that, you should not practice in a tense manner either—both body and mind should be relaxed. And therein lies the skill of a genuine practitioner: to practice without tension and yet seamlessly. Like water that flows naturally and continuously, there should be no gaps in keeping the huatou before yourself. Depending on your strength and stamina, you may be like a small stream or a great river. Either way, the key is to relax and, at the same time, to have great urgency. And there must be earnestness concerning the matter of life and death. This is how you investigate Chan.

Do not pressure yourself to the extent of harming yourself. The job of the Dharma teachers here is to set the proper tone in the Chan Hall. You do your part, and they will do theirs. Up to now they have been rather kind. They have been lenient to those who have been a little lax, even though you needed to be wakened from your daydreams. Starting today they will be stricter. For those who are hazy, or drowsy, and those who are watching movies inside their head, the Dharma teachers will come around and help you snap out of it.

A more forceful approach can be quite effective during walking meditation. A retreat monitor may suddenly confront you and shout, "Where is this *wu*? Is it in your mouth? In your feet? In your heart?" The truth is that your whole being should be *wu*. But the monitor will demand that you tell him where *wu* is. To be ready when the monitor tries to tease *wu* out of you, you must investigate *wu* without interruption. If you feel the need to answer when asked "Where is *wu*?" that would be deluded thinking. On the other hand your investigation should arouse the sense that there is no answer to *wu*. If you perceive that everything is just *wu*, don't stop there, as you still do not know what *wu* itself is. "What is *wu*?" Because you cannot answer, a doubt will arise. So being asked about *wu* is not meant to tease an answer out of you, but to arouse doubt in you.

Venerable Guo Jun (one of the Dharma teachers at the retreat) told me he has not shouted at anyone yet. If he does, please do not take it personally; he is just arousing you to practice harder. On the other hand please don't wait for him to shout at you as that would only deflate the power of his words. What you *should* be doing is continuously investigating *wu* and generating the doubt sensation.

To finish this evening, let's take a few more lines of Dahui's discourse:

> Have you not heard the words of the ancient worthy ones that all the Dharma spoken by the Buddha is for the purpose of delivering all kinds of minds? If there's no mind, of what use is all the Dharma?

Dahui is saying that all the devices for teaching Dharma are really antidotes for the delusions of sentient beings. How do you use Dharma to cut off delusions? I have already said that the so-called severing of delusions is merely an expedient teaching, because there is no need to sever deluded thinking. As long as wandering thoughts do not hold you captive, as long as you are not moved by them, you will have already transformed them into prajna, the essence of wisdom. If the workings of the mind leave no imprint on you, you can freely use them in the service of wisdom. If you are not affected by wandering thoughts, they can work for you, and this is how to sever delusion.

Use All Circumstances as Points of Entry

Let's continue our commentary on Dahui's discourse:

> Most of the literati who study this path seek after quick results. Before the master even opens his mouth to speak, these people will have already formulated a conceptual understanding with their minds, thoughts, and perceptions. When obstructions creep up on them, they lose all control; they become busy with their hands and feet without having anything to hold on to. They don't know that it is actually their conceptual understanding that will take them to King Yama to receive the blows of the iron rod and swallow the blazing iron ball. The person who seeks after quick results is none other than you. And so it is said that those who wish to acquire it will lose it. Those who try to be meticulous will end up being more negligent. The tathagata considers such people pitiable.

This passage points out the tendency among some intellectuals to be eager for results, looking for shortcuts to enlightenment. These intellectuals are quick with witty turns of phrase, and interpret and analyze what they hear or read, looking for hidden meanings. They forget that Buddhadharma is meant to respond to the needs of sentient beings by prescribing an antidote. Instead many prefer to analyze the medicine instead of just taking it. I have met intellectuals who like to discuss Buddhism, but when I suggest that a retreat would help their practice, they often say something like, "Shifu, I've read your books, and coming on retreat would be just hearing those words all over." To such people Chan seems to be mostly about ideas, but the whole point of Chan is to free oneself from concepts. Without engaging in actual practice, it is very difficult to get in touch with the essence of life. That is something that mere words cannot do. To resolve the question of birth and death, one has to directly perceive their essential nature. The understanding gained from words is useful up to a point, but real-life issues can only be resolved by practice.

All the words of the Chan masters point to the one reality of practice. To engage the huatou is to bring forth *wu* in daily life, to detach from self-attachment, speculation, and analysis. This is quite different from gaining conceptual understanding of Dharma. A Chan master will not necessarily explain things clearly, but all of his or her words point to using a Chan method. For Dahui, the method is to use *wu* to break down the barriers to perceiving one's essential nature. There's no denying that reading books on Chan can be useful; it may help one to live a relatively happy and peaceful life. But to actually gain a genuine entry into the practice just through reading is rare. Mere conceptual understanding will not penetrate to the core of your being. You need to engage a method of practice that will allow you to shatter the barrier and perceive directly the wellspring of your being. Otherwise, if you rely on analysis and reasoning, when you confront King Yama, the demon of death, your mind will be in chaos.

Once, an intellectual complimented me on having written many books and given many lectures. He said I was able to do this because I was very intelligent, adding that I had chosen the right path for myself, because I had a quick wit. Unlike others, he said, who, no matter how many books they read or koans they study, are still baffled. In other words, this gentleman reduced me to being a quick-witted smarty. He was also implying that only smart people are able to study Chan and get something out of it. As I saw it, by making these observations, this person revealed himself to be one of the literati.

I told him, "I am not the person that you think I am; in fact I consider myself slow. It is not as if the koans just flow from my mind; there are many I still do not understand. For these reasons, I very earnestly need to practice." With witty people, if you raise one issue, they will multiply it by a hundredfold. Dahui was particularly critical of elites who thought they understood Buddhadharma after one reading, deceiving themselves as to their fundamental true nature, their original face. They mistook the Chan rhetoric for the true Chan. They took these flashes of light and the sounds as Chan itself. In fact these are altered states outside the door of Chan, the experience of light and ease or some sort of insight. These situations are typically very accessible to people with keen wit. They can read some Dharma and immediately gain some insight, thinking they have grasped the knob to the door of Chan. Actually they're still running in circles outside the door, involving themselves with these so-called experiences. The only way for them to actually penetrate the Chan door would be to take up *wu*. So, Dahui often told these men that it was precisely because of their overbearing knowledge that they should practice *wu*.

Last night Ven. Guo Jun told me one of you had reached the unified state. As you may recall, I identified three states in huatou practice: the concentrated state, the unified state, and the state of no-mind. In the concentrated state, your wandering thoughts and your huatou are intermingled; discursive thinking rises and falls, but the huatou is still there for you to pick up; it still functions actively. In that sense, in the concentrated state, both wandering thoughts and the huatou are simultaneously present.

In the unified state, body, mind, environment, and all the burdens that come with them have ceased and only the huatou remains. The method is still there, but you don't feel burdened anymore. Please note that this state has its own variations in depth and range of experience. But the unified state is not enough if the doubt sensation is not present; therefore, you must still give rise to doubt. When the doubt sensation arises, you must then push on with great urgency so that the doubt sensation becomes a great mass of doubt. Only when this great mass of doubt is shattered will you reach no-mind, the third state.

Today I encouraged Ven. Guo Jun to push you folks harder. Perhaps one of you, upon hearing him roar, "What is *wu*?" may respond by suddenly shattering your great ball of doubt. Depending on whether this shattering is small or great, you may or may not experience wisdom, but even a glimpse of wisdom can be considered a kind of enlightenment. Whatever your state, if your practice is grounded in *wu*, you will always find your way back to *wu*; grounded in *wu*, you can gain an entry wherever you may be. All states are opportunities to practice. Do not think that the only benefit of practice is to gain awakening. When you can use all circumstances as entry points to practice, you will have wealth you can use in daily life. However, please be aware of a kind of false enlightenment where you suddenly feel you have been released and there is nothing more you need to do. It is precisely at that point that you should pick up the method. So, please put all your effort into the practice.

Returning Home to Your Original Place

Tonight I will conclude my commentary on Master Dahui's text:

In recent times many literati desire to study this path, yet their hearts are not pure; their sickness comes from the fact that poison has entered their hearts. When poison enters the heart, you'll be caught up with whatever you encounter. Being caught up with whatever you encounter, your attachment to the view of the self will grow. As the view of the self increases, all you see and hear will be the shortcomings of other people and you will not be able to take the backward step and briefly examine yourself. "Day by day, after leaving my bed in the morning, what benefit have I brought to myself or others?" One who is able to self-examine like this is called a wise person.

This passage speaks of practitioners with acute wits who can quickly size up a situation. This can be a problem if they are not able to discard wandering thoughts while single-mindedly bringing forth the huatou. Instead, they bring forth venom—criticisms, comparisons, jealousy, and so on. Of these people, Dahui says, "Poison has entered their hearts." People with an impure mind see shortcomings, problems, and weaknesses in other people, while not examining themselves. Instead, in Dahui's words, they should ask, "Day by day, after leaving my bed in the morning, what benefit have I brought to myself or others?" If they can do this, they truly have a chance to enter the path, but wallowing in critical thoughts is not how practice works.

Dahui's view is in accordance with that of the sixth patriarch Huineng, who said that one who is on the path does not see fault in others. Does this mean that we should not respond to wrongs that we see? Because people do not always perceive things the same way, we need to take care how we respond. Getting people to recognize their faults takes skill. There are times we can raise the issue directly, but at other times we have to be circumspect. But if we can get people to recognize their errors without being confrontational, that is skillful as well as compassionate.

I had a disciple who was fond of cottage cheese, and at breakfast he would always place the container in front of himself. Someone complained to me about this, and I said, "Well, he may not perceive himself as being selfish; maybe he just likes cottage cheese. Instead of being critical, you should help him by reminding him to be more sharing." For the disciple who was complaining, it was especially vexing since he made the criticism behind the other's back. In this case it was the complainer who had poison in his heart. So having a tendency to see wrongs in others can be poison in your heart, especially if you have to hold it in. It is better to engage in self-examination through single-minded use of the method.

I want to conclude my commentary on Dahui's discourse:

Master Zhaozhou once said, "As for this old monk, besides the two mealtimes of the day when he uses his mind in a complex manner, there are no other occasions where it requires his mind to be complicated." You may wonder where this old fellow is at. If you can recognize his original face, then you can say such things like "Walking is Chan; sitting is Chan; whether talking, silent, active, or still, everything is at peace." If you are unable to be like this, then you better at all times take the backward step and carefully examine that which is under your own feet. Is it really possible to really know another person's strengths or weaknesses, or to judge whether he or she is an ordinary person or a saint, whether things are truly existent or empty? Pushing and exhausting this self-investigation from one situation to the next until there's nowhere you can drive this questioning, like a mouse getting stuck on the horn of a bull, suddenly you must sever this cunning mind. This is a state where all things will solidify, a place where you can return home and finally firmly sit in peace.

Dahui quotes Master Zhaozhou who says that, aside from the two mealtimes a day, he has no need to use his mind in a complex manner. We should not think that Zhaozhou is not mindful when he is eating. That is not the meaning here, and certainly it is not the same as poison entering one's heart. It is just that he is aware of what he is eating and is mindful of it. This runs against conventional thinking: if you can be single-minded all day, why should eating be complicated? But we should not be tricked by Master Zhaozhou—just like his saying that a dog does not have buddha-nature. So if, like me, you don't understand it, you can just use it as a gong'an and investigate it.

Dahui says, "You may wonder where this old fellow is at," and goes on to say that if someone can meet Zhaozhou face-to-face and testify to the master's realization of his original face, then such a person is allowed to say, "Eating is Chan; walking is Chan; standing is Chan; lying down is Chan." Surely it is a difficult state to attain where you can hold on to the method without straying from your original face. Such a person would be enlightened and in accord with awakened mind. If you cannot be like this, then you should reflect on how you are carrying yourself throughout the day. What have you done that is of use to yourself or others? And if you can't find anything, then you had better investigate Chan, because how can we know what other people are like, how can we assess other people's strengths and weaknesses? Who are we to say that other people are saints and sages or just ordinary people and whether or not they have "gotten it?" So engaging in this kind of self-reflection is what a practitioner should do.

However if you allow poison to enter your heart by being very critical, assessing and judging other people's goodness and short-comings, then it is like cornering yourself on the point of an ox's horn. This is a Chan saying meaning there is no way out. Cornering yourself like that is certainly not practice. So, as soon as you dis-cover that poison has entered your heart, immediately cut off this cunning mind, this mind of a thief. When you can truly cut off this cunning mind, then it will be like returning home to your original place, where you can firmly rest at peace.

Glossary

Agama: (Skt., "what has been handed down") The collection of sutras and other scriptures forming part of the Sanskrit canon of early Buddhism. The agamas correspond to the Nikayas, which were written in Pali. Within the Mahayana tradition the agamas stand apart from the later Mahayana sutras also written in Sanskrit, for which there are no Pali counterparts. The agamas are part of the second of the Tripitaka, the Sutras. *See also* **Tripitaka.**

Amitabha: (Skt.; Chin., Amituofo) The Buddha of the Western Paradise, who vowed to deliver sentient beings to the Pure Land if they recited his name. This practice is the basis of the Pure Land sects of China and Japan.

Arhat: (Skt., "noble one" or "worthy one") One who has fulfilled the practice and has attained liberation from samsara, the cycle of birth and death. Referred to as "one who has no more to learn," the arhat has become liberated from all desires and defilements, and has attained nirvana. As such, the arhat is no longer subject to rebirth. *See also* **Bodhisattva, Nirvana, Samsara.**

Bodhichitta: (Skt., "awakened mind," or "*bodhi*-mind") A central idea in Mahayana Buddhism, with various meanings: (1) the altruistic mind of enlightenment, which aspires to buddhahood for the sake of helping sentient beings; (2) the genuine actualization of enlightenment, awakening to the true nature of reality and the loftiness of buddhahood; (3) selfless action. The last meaning, selfless action, is very important but often overlooked. Arousing bodhichitta is the first step in establishing oneself on the bodhisattva path. *See also* **Bodhisattva.**

Bodhidharma: (d. 536?) Indian monk who traveled to China to teach his version of enlightenment through direct contemplation of the mind. He later was regarded as the founder of the Chinese Chan traditions of Buddhism.

*Bodhi-*mind: *See* **Bodhichitta.**

Bodhisattva: (Skt., "awakened being" or "enlightened being") The model ideal of the Mahayana tradition of Buddhism, one who practices for the sake of sentient beings, as opposed to practicing for one's own liberation. In this sense, the bodhisattva path is contrasted with that of the arhat. *See also* **Arhat, Bodhichitta, Four Great Vows.**

Buddhadharma: (Skt., "truth of the Buddha") Collectively, the Dharma teachings of the Buddha. The Dharma should not be understood as a fixed set of doctrines. Thus the Buddha said, "The Dharma has no fixed Dharma." Essentially, the Buddha taught in response to the different dispositions of sentient beings.

Caodong: (Chin., pinyin) Line of Chinese Buddhism named after its two founders, Master Caoshan and Master Dongshan, hence the name "Caodong." The Caodong line emphasizes the practice of Silent Illumination (J., *shikantaza*), although practices such as gong'an and huatou are also common. Along with the Linji (J., Rinzai), the Caodong (J., Soto) line is one of the two major surviving lines of Chan or Zen Buddhism. *See also* **Linji.**

Chan: (Chin., transliteration of the Sanskrit *dhyana* ["meditation"]; J., Zen) Chinese tradition of Buddhism said to be founded by the monk Bodhidharma around the sixth century. The tradition is characterized by its teaching of enlightenment through direct experience of the nature of mind, or buddha-nature, as described in the often-quoted phrase, "A special teaching outside the scriptures, pointing directly to the mind."

Deva: (Skt., "shining one") A deity who inhabits the celestial realm of rebirth.

Dharma: (Skt., "truth" or "law") *See* **Buddhadharma.**

Fashi: (Chin., "Dharma teacher") Honorific for an accomplished teacher of the Dharma.

Five Precepts: Guidelines to ethical and moral behavior that Buddhists vow to uphold. The precepts are not to kill, not to steal, not to engage in sexual misconduct, not to lie, and not to consume intoxicants. The Five Precepts are frequently taken as part of taking refuge. *See also* **Taking Refuge.**

Four Great Vows: Part of the daily liturgy in Chan temples; also taken as part of the bodhisattva precepts ceremony. The Four Great Vows of the bodhisattva are:

I vow to deliver all sentient beings.
I vow to cut off endless vexations.
I vow to master all approaches to the Dharma.
I vow to attain supreme buddhahood.

See also **Bodhisattva.**

Gong'an: (Chin., "public case"; J., *koan*) A saying or anecdote from the records of the Chan masters that is used as a means of "investigating the nature of enlightened mind." The purpose of the exercise is to focus the mind and create a mass of doubt, to the point that all attachments and dualistic thinking are dropped and the practitioner experiences a breakthrough—the direct perception of Buddhist emptiness. In Chan, gong'an practice is closely associated with the practice of huatou. *See also* **Huatou.**

Huatou: (Chin., "head of a thought"; J., *wato*) A practice in which one meditatively investigates a question, such as "What is your original face?", in order to give rise to a doubt mass that can lead to a realization of emptiness. The method can only be penetrated if the practitioner abandons conceptual and discriminating mind while practicing the huatou. In Chan, huatou practice is closely associated with the practice of gong'an. *See also* **Gong'an.**

Incense Board: A thin, flat wooden board that is sometimes used by a Chan master or meditation monitor to strike the shoulders of a practitioner in order to spur the sitter to more diligent effort or simply to stir them from drowsiness. In more modern times, the use of the incense board (J., *kyosaku*) has become more of a voluntary option in which the sitter raises his or her hand to ask to be struck on the shoulders.

Koan: *See* **Gong'an.**

Linji: (d. ca. 866–867) (J., Rinzai) Master Linji is the founder of the Chan sect that bears his name. The Linji sect was characterized by its emphasis on meditation and the use of gong'an and huatou methods to create a "doubt mass" in the mind of the practitioner. The resolution of the doubt mass is an essential step toward realizing enlightenment. The Linji sect is one of two remaining Chan sects, the other being the Caodong (J., Soto). *See also* **Caodong.**

Mahayana: (Skt., "great vehicle") Name applied to the later tradition of Buddhism based on the teachings of the Middle Way enunciated by the Indian scholar Nagarjuna. The Mahayana path is essentially the path of the bodhisattvas, who defer their own enlightenment in order to deliver sentient beings. *See also* **Bodhisattva, Middle Way.**

Mara: (Skt.) 1) Refers to the Lord of Evil, or the Lord of the Dead. 2) In another context, Mara is the demonic spirit who unsuccessfully tried to seduce Shakyamuni from his dedicated practice. 3) On a more mundane level, Buddhist teachers sometimes refer to various kinds of distractions from true practice as maras, or "demonic influences."

Middle Way: 1) Refers to the Buddha's teaching that the proper path is to avoid either extreme of self-imposed suffering in asceticism, or indulgence in desire and attachments. 2) Philosophically, the Middle Way refers to the teaching of the Madhyamaka tradition of Buddhism (ca. 5th century) in which the true practitioner avoids the dual errors of nihilism, in which nothing exists, and eternalism, in which phenomena have independent and durable existence.

Nikaya: (Skt.) Collection of Buddhist sutras in the Pali canon of early Buddhism.

Nirvana: (Skt., "extinction") The state of having overcome all mental defilements and of being liberated from the cycle of birth and death (samsara), that is to say, when all worldly attachments and desires have been "extinguished." Correspondingly, nirvana is the state of being free from karma, the chain of cause and effect. *See also* **Parinirvana, Samsara.**

Original Face: In the Chinese Chan tradition, a metaphor for one's original buddha-nature.

Parinirvana: (Skt., "total extinction") A term synonymous with "nirvana," but also connoting the act of passing into nirvana through death. The term also refers to the death of the Buddha and his passing into nirvana. It may also refer to the death of a monastic. *See also* **Nirvana.**

Patriarch: In the context of Chan or Zen Buddhism, an honorific referring to one of the six teachers considered to be the founding ancestors of the Chan or Zen tradition. Beginning with the putatively Indian (some say Central Asian) monk Bodhidharma (d. 536?), the other five are Chinese. In chronological order they are Huike (487–593), Sengcan (d. 606), Daoxin (580–651), Hongren (602–675), and Huineng (638–713).

Prajnaparamita: (Skt., "wisdom that reaches the other shore") (1) Transcendent wisdom. (2) The term also refers to the *Mahaprajnaparamita Sutra,* a series of some forty Mahayana sutras on the central topic of prajna, or wisdom. Today, the best-known sutras from the set are the *Heart Sutra* and the *Diamond Sutra*.

Samadhi: (Skt., "make firm") In general, refers to a state of meditative absorption in which one has reached a degree of concentration where the sense of time is foreshortened or even temporarily lost. Someone in samadhi for hours, upon coming out of samadhi, may think only a few moments have passed. There are many levels of samadhi, from shallow to deep enlightenment. In Buddhism, samadhi is not equated with enlightenment so long as the practitioner still retains a sense of self. In this book, samadhi is understood as the inseparability of concentration and wisdom. Master Sheng Yen defines Silent Illumination as a form of samadhi.

Samsara: (Skt., "journeying") The cycle of birth and death in which ordinary unenlightened sentient beings are deeply immersed. There are three realms within samsara: the desire realm, the form realm, and the formless realm. Ordinary sentient beings, including humans, inhabit the desire realm. To transcend samsara is to enter nirvana, although to the thoroughly enlightened, samsara and nirvana are not different realms—they are one and the same. *See also* **Nirvana.**

Sentient Being: Not restricted to human beings, the term includes all living things that are capable of sensation, and therefore suffering.

Skandha: (Skt., "heap" or "aggregate") The constituents of a sentient being's experience of the world. The five skandhas are form, sensation, perception, volition, and consciousness. The first skandha of form is the material component; the other four are mental in nature. Operating together, the five skandhas create the illusion of separate existence and the notion of self or ego.

Sutra: (Skt., "thread") Any of the sermons attributed to the historical Buddha, Shakyamuni. Collectively, the Sutras are one part of the Tripitaka, "three baskets," of teachings, of which the other two are the Vinaya and the Abhidharma. *See also* **Agama, Tripitaka.**

Taking Refuge: A ceremony in which devotees take refuge in the so-called Three Jewels: the Buddha, the Dharma, and the Sangha. The Buddha-jewel is the historical buddha and founding teacher, Shakyamuni; the Dharma-jewel is, collectively, the teachings of the Buddha. The Sangha-jewel consists of the community of monks and nuns, as well as the laity. By taking refuge, devotees declare themselves to be followers of the Buddhist path.

Tripitaka: (Skt., "three baskets") The canon of the Buddhist scriptures consisting of three categories: the Vinaya (Skt., "precepts"), the Sutras (Skt., "sermons [of the Buddha]"), and the Abhidharma (Skt., "concerning dharmas").

True Suchness: English approximation of the Sanskrit "tathata" (and also "tathagatagarbha"), referring to the absolute true nature of all things, or buddha-nature.

Zendo: (J.) In Japanese Zen, the meditation hall, the place where Zen is practiced. In Chan, the equivalent name would be "Chan Hall."

Sources

This section identifies each chapter in this book in terms of the retreat during which the lecture was given. The four retreats are arbitrarily named R1–R4, with their inclusive dates. All four retreats were given at the Dharma Drum Retreat Center in Pine Bush, New York.

The Retreats:

R1: 25 Dec. 1998–1 Jan. 1999
R2: 29 May 1999–6 June 1999
R3: 24 Dec. 1999–1 Jan. 2000
R4: 24 Nov. 2006–2 Dec. 2006

Part One: Exposition of the Huatou Method

THE HUATOU METHOD

R2: Discovering Huatou
R2: Meditating on the Breath
R2: Reciting a Buddha's Name

R3: To Know Yourself
R2: Like the Two Wings of a Bird
R4: "What is *Wu?*"
R3: Stages of Huatou Practice
R4: Investigating Huatou
R2: Generating the Doubt Sensation
R3: Body and Mind Phenomena
R4: The Meaning of Huatou Practice
R3: Direct Contemplation

CULTIVATION

R2: The Meaning of Cultivation
R2: When Will You Have Another Opportunity?
R2: Faith in Mind
R4: Light and Sound Outside the Gate
R3: Upholding the Precepts
R2: Diligence and Humility
R2: Repentance
R4: Confidence, Determination, and Long-Enduring Mind

THE MIDDLE WAY

R2: Practice and the Middle Way
R2: Huatou and the Middle Way
R3: Fundamental Ignorance
R3: Correct Views
R2: Bodhichitta and Renunciation
R2: The Four Great Vows
R3: Attitudes for Practicing Chan
R4: Emptying the Heart
R3: Emptiness

Sources

Part Two: Commentaries on Huatou Practice

THE ESSENTIALS OF PRACTICE AND
ENLIGHTENTMENT FOR BEGINNERS

R1: The Fragility of Life
R1: Points on Technique
R1: Using the Vajra Sword to Kill Delusions
R1: Giving Rise to the Doubt Sensation
R1: Beginner's Mind
R1: Practicing *Mu* at Twenty-seven below Zero
R1: Doing Battle with the Ten Thousand Enemies

AN EXCERPT FROM
Impetus to Pass through the Chan Gate

R2: Your Virtuous Karmic Potential
R2: The Difficulty of Obtaining a Human Birth
R2: Beyond Words and Language
R2: Mind and Body: Two Aspects of Self
R2: Karmic Consciousness
R2: Shattering the Great Doubt
R2: The Three Stages of Doubt
R2: The Great Doubt in Daily Life
R2: At the Threshold of Hell
R2: The Sword of Wisdom
R2: Diligence

BUDDHA IS MEDICINE
FOR SENTIENT BEINGS

R3: Affirming the Self
R3: To Manifest Wisdom

191

R3: *Wu* and Buddha-Nature
R3: Buddhas and Maras
R3: To Empty the Myriad Things
R3: True Suchness
R3: Stages on the Path of Enlightenment

THE GREAT MATTER OF BIRTH AND DEATH

R4: The Great Matter of Birth and Death
R4: The Place Where Buddhas Are Chosen
R4: Use All Circumstances as Points of Entry
R4: Returning Home to Your Original Place

Index